DRAW **50** ALIENS, UFOs, GALAXY GHOULS, MILKY WAY MARAUDERS, AND OTHER EXTRATERRESTRIAL CREATURES

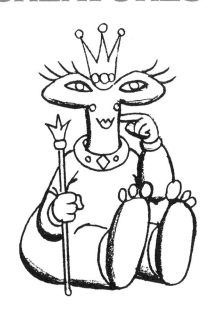

BOOKS IN THIS SERIES

DRAW 50 ALIENS, UFOs, GALAXY GHOULS, MILKY WAY MARAUDERS, AND OTHER EXTRATERRESTRIAL CREATURES

Lee J. Ames
with Ric Estrada

DOUBLEDAY

NEW YORK LONDON TORONTO SYDNEY AUCKLAND

PUBLISHED BY DOUBLEDAY
a division of Bantam Doubleday Dell Publishing Group, Inc.
1540 Broadway, New York, New York 10036

DOUBLEDAY and the portrayal of an anchor with a dolphin are trademarks of Doubleday,
a division of Bantam Doubleday Dell Publishing Group, Inc.

Library of Congress Cataloging-in-Publication Data applied for.

ISBN 0-385-49144-1
Copyright © 1998 by Lee J. Ames with Ric Estrada

For Loretta
and our eight wonders:
Aaron
Marc
Aleli
Bekah
Seth
Jeremy
Ethan
Hannah
and of course, Zilia
(Also a wonder!)

None of the above are extraterrestrial,
but all are out of this world!

My work includes children's book illustrations, articles for *Dance* magazine, *Spandauer Volksblatt* and *Sonne*, ghosting the *Flash Gordon* and *Spider Man* comic strips, political cartooning, innumerable comic books (*Superman*, *Batman*, *Wonder Woman*, *Sgt. Rock*, countless superheroes) and, in recent years, lots of TV advertising storyboards (Kodak, Breck, Alpo, U.S. Armed Forces, etc.) and cartoon animation for Hanna-Barbera, Warner Bros., DreamWorks and, currently, for Sony–Columbia–Tri-Star.

But my greatest adventure is my family—a wonderful wife and nine magnificent children bursting with talents and ambition.

I hope you enjoy drawing these extraterrestrial goonies as much as my good friend Lee Ames and I enjoyed dreaming them up.

Happy sketching!!!

—RIC ESTRADA

To the Reader

When you start working, use clean white bond paper or drawing paper and a pencil with moderately soft lead (HB or No. 2). Keep a kneaded eraser handy (available at art supply stores). Choose the alien you want to draw. Try to imagine the finished drawing on the drawing area. Then visualize the first steps so that the finished picture will nicely fill the page—not too large, not too small. Now, very lightly and very carefully, sketch out the first step. (These first steps are indicated in color for clarity. You can use a colored pencil crayon here if you prefer *or* a regular pencil.) Next, very lightly and carefully, add the second step, the third step, and so on. As you go along, study not only the lines but the spaces between the lines. Remember, the first steps must be sketched with the greatest care. A mistake here could ruin your final drawing.

As you work, it's a good idea, from time to time, to hold a mirror to your sketch. The image in the mirror frequently shows distortion you might not recognize otherwise.

In the book you will notice that the new step additions (in color) are printed darker so they can be clearly identified. But be sure to keep all of your construction steps very light. Here's where the kneaded eraser can be useful. You can lighten a pencil stroke that is too dark by pressing on it with the eraser.

When you've completed all the light steps, and when you're sure you have everything the way you want it, finish your drawing with firm, strong pencil strokes. If you like, you can go over this with India ink (applied with a fine brush or pen) or a permanent fine-tipped ballpoint pen or a felt-tipped marker. When thoroughly dry, you can then rub the kneaded eraser over the entire surface to clean out all the underlying pencil marks.

Remember, if your first attempts at drawing do not turn out the way you'd like, it's important to *keep trying*. Your efforts will eventually pay off and you'll be pleased and surprised at what you can accomplish. I sincerely hope, as you follow our techniques, that your skills will improve. Following the way Ric and I work and then exercising your thinking tools can open the door to your own creativity. We hope you will enjoy drawing our extraterrestrial friends.

LEE J. AMES

DRAW 50 ALIENS, UFOs, GALAXY GHOULS, MILKY WAY MARAUDERS, AND OTHER EXTRATERRESTRIAL CREATURES

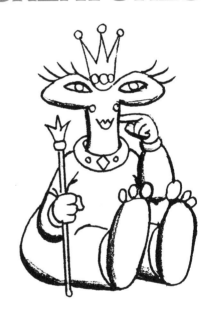

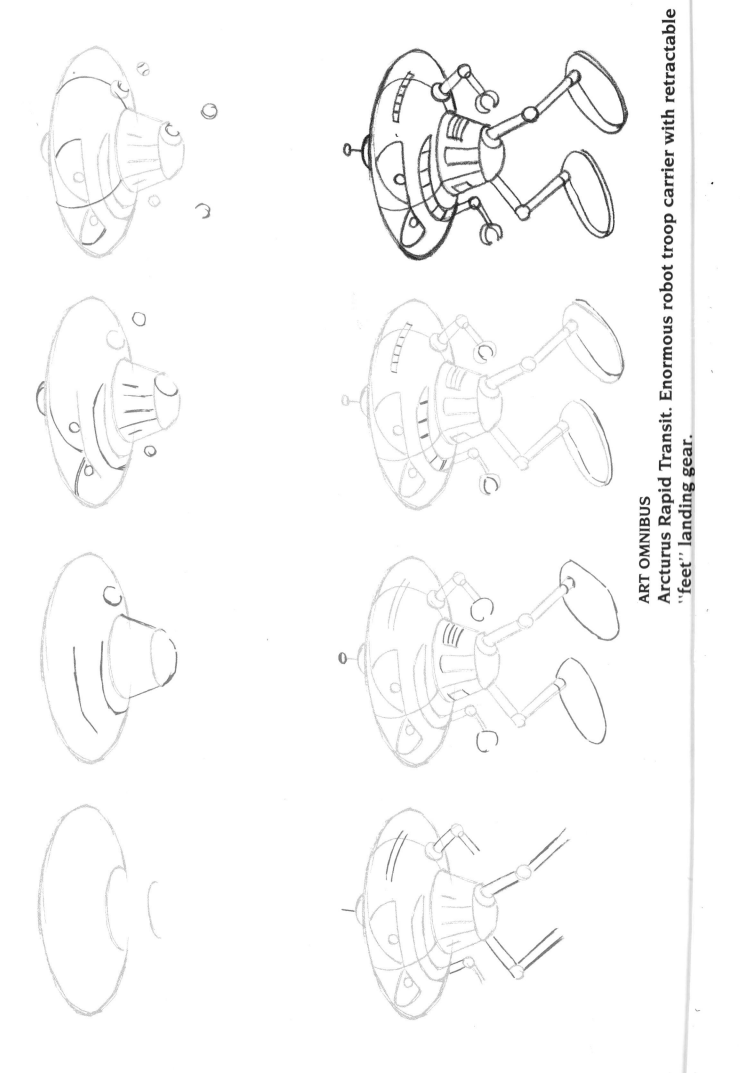

ART OMNIBUS

Arcturus Rapid Transit. Enormous robot troop carrier with retractable "feet" landing gear.

UFOs

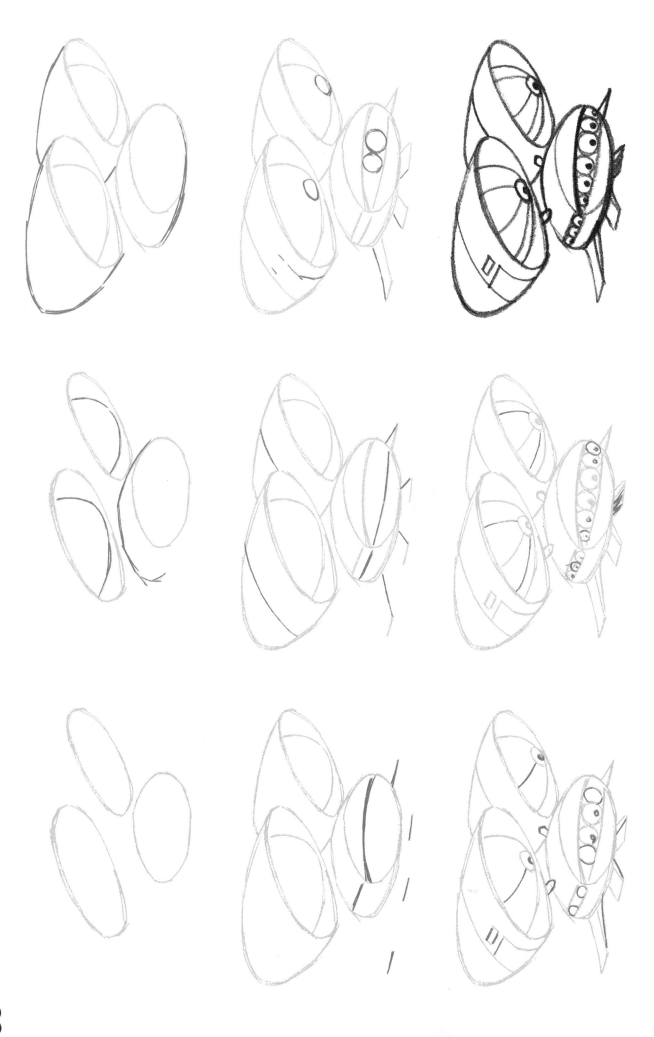

PUDDDEL

Primary Ultra 3 Dimensional Elevator, propelled by enormous twin laser beamatrons.

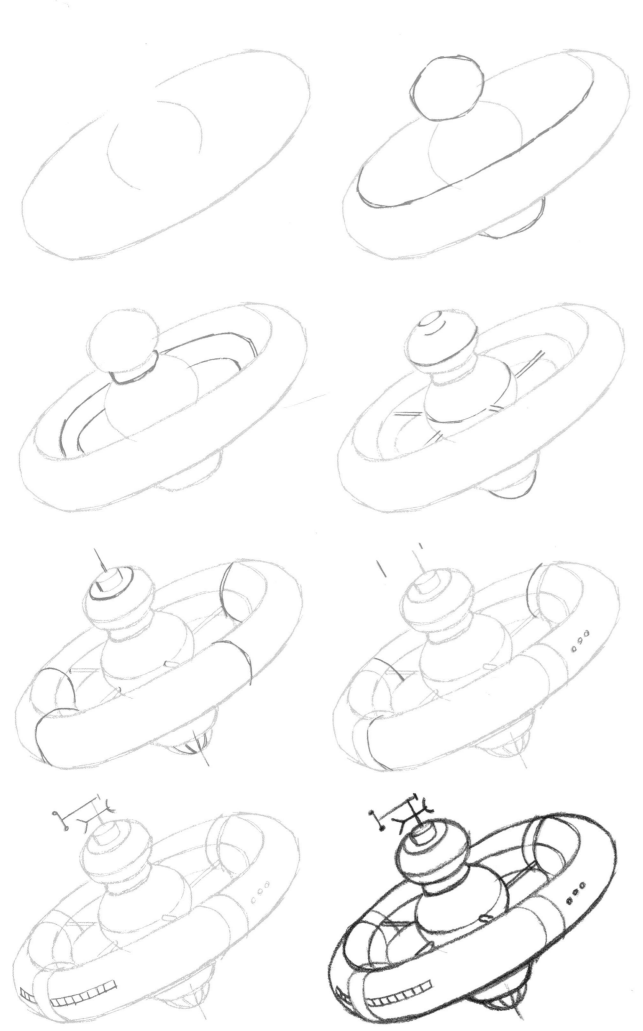

MUDDDDEL

Major Ultra 4th Dimensional Elevator. Transports population of two to three villages.

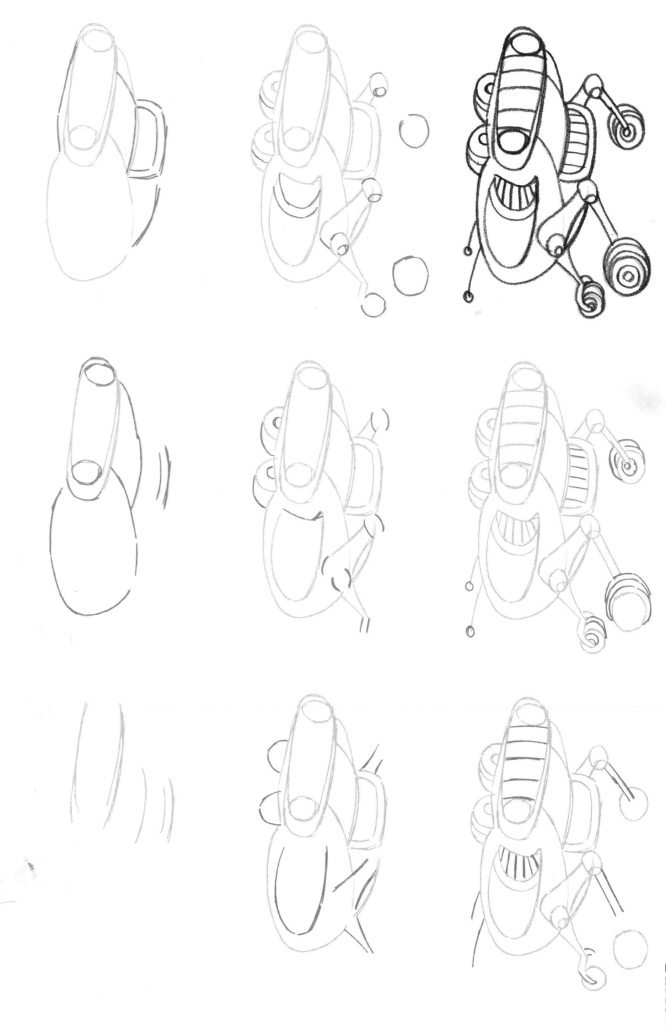

PST MODULE

Principal Stellar Transportation. Official personnel carrier with huge, rolling landing gear.

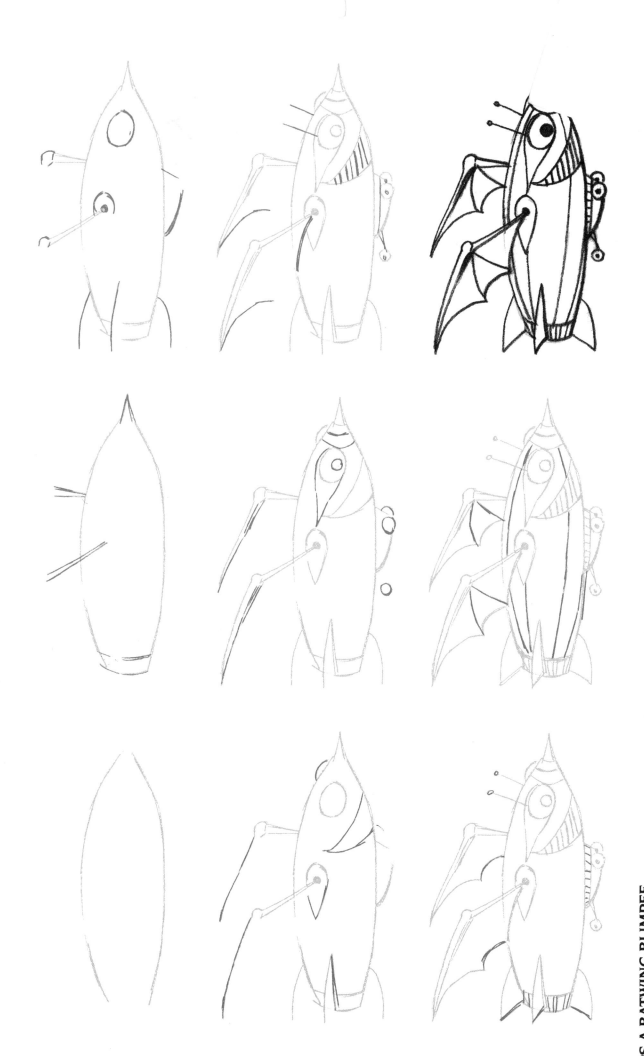

IOT-PS A BATWING BLIMPEE
An Inter-Orbit Ten Passenger Shuttle yet to be discovered.

THE GREYS

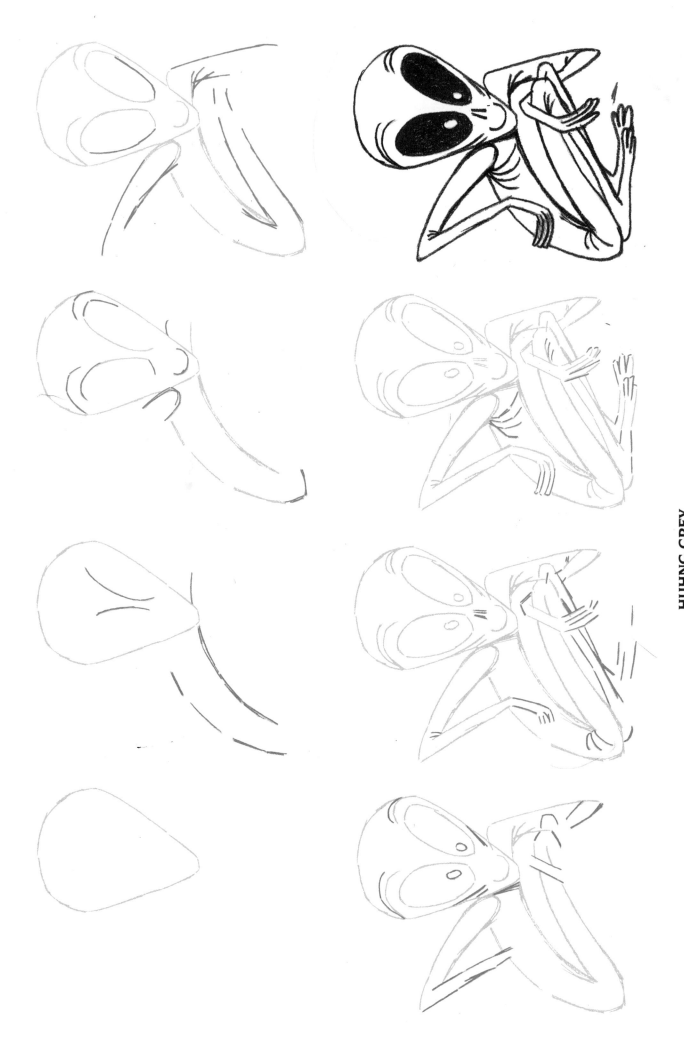

HUHNG GREY
Common gaunt Grey spotted near Route 375 in Arizona. Home unknown.

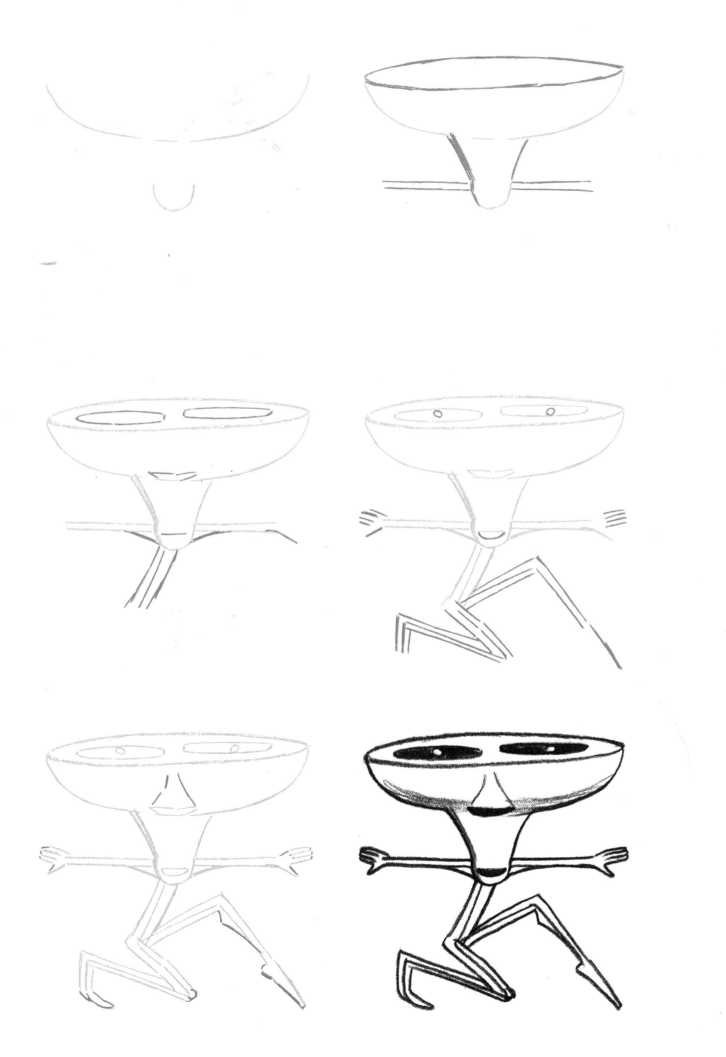

LEV EL HEDDID
Sensible, even-tempered visitor from vicinity of Fum al Samakah.

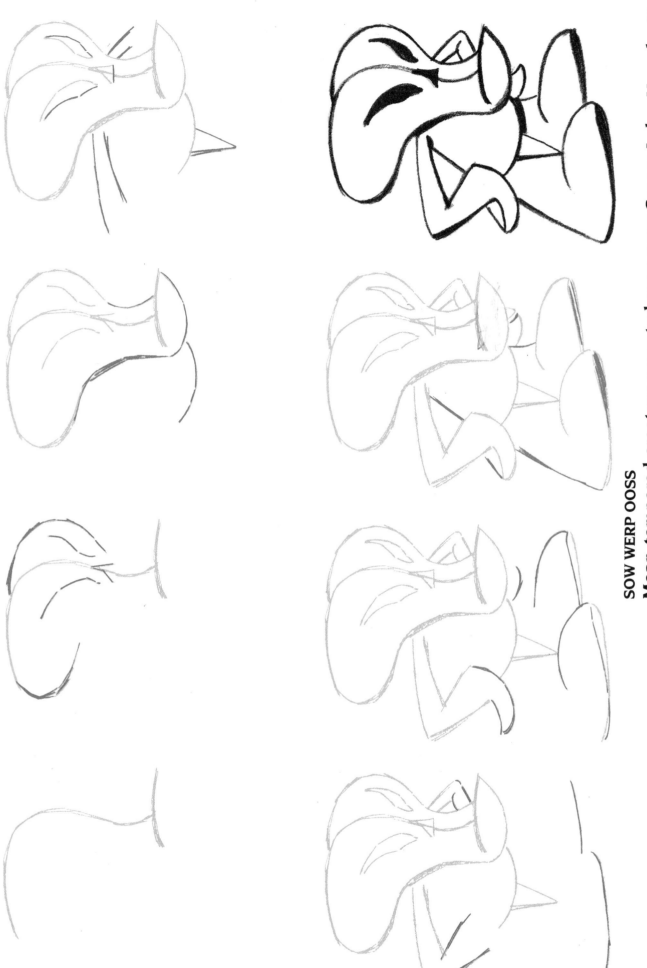

SOW WERP OOSS
Mean-tempered creature reported seen near Groom Lake, Nevada. Home unknown.

UFOs

PUDDDEL
Primary Ultra 3 Dimensional Elevator, propelled by enormous twin laser
beamatrons.

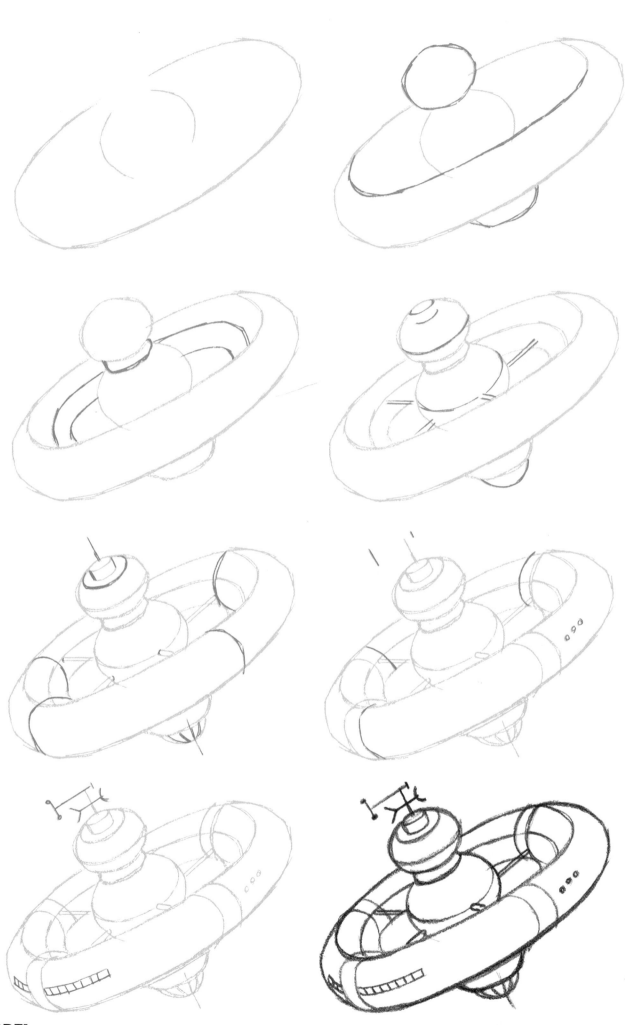

MUDDDDEL

Major Ultra 4th Dimensional Elevator. Transports population of two to three villages.

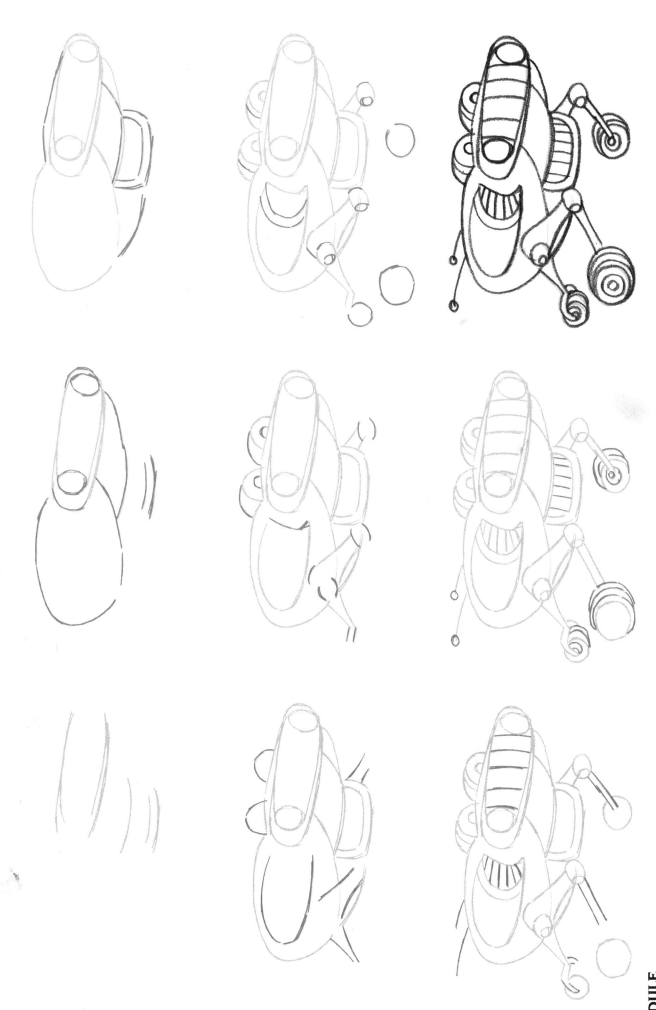

PST MODULE
**Principal Stellar Transportation. Official personnel carrier with huge,
rolling landing gear.**

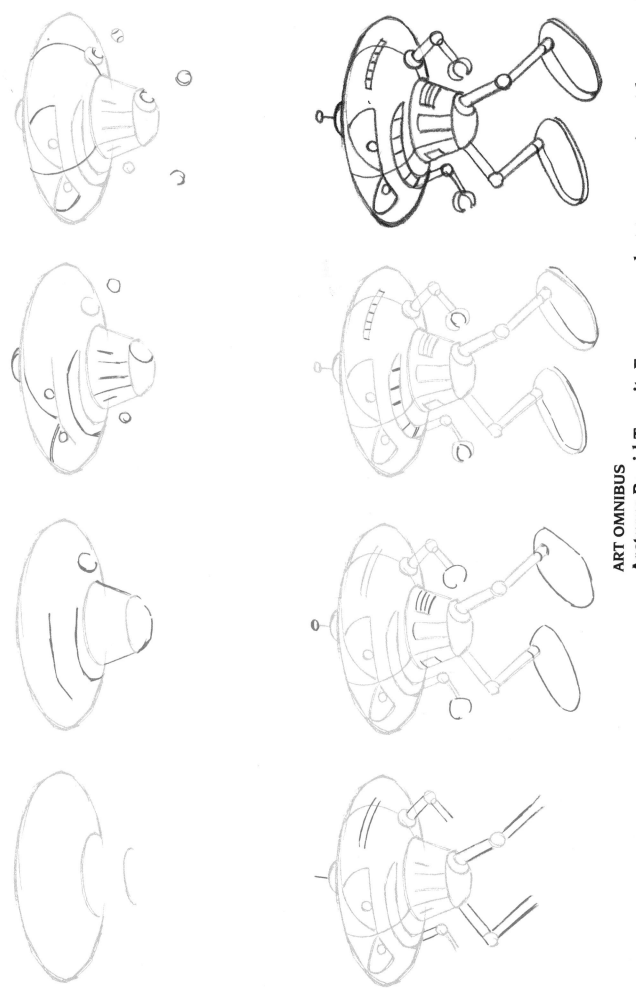

ART OMNIBUS
Arcturus Rapid Transit. Enormous robot troop carrier with retractable "feet" landing gear.

THE GREYS

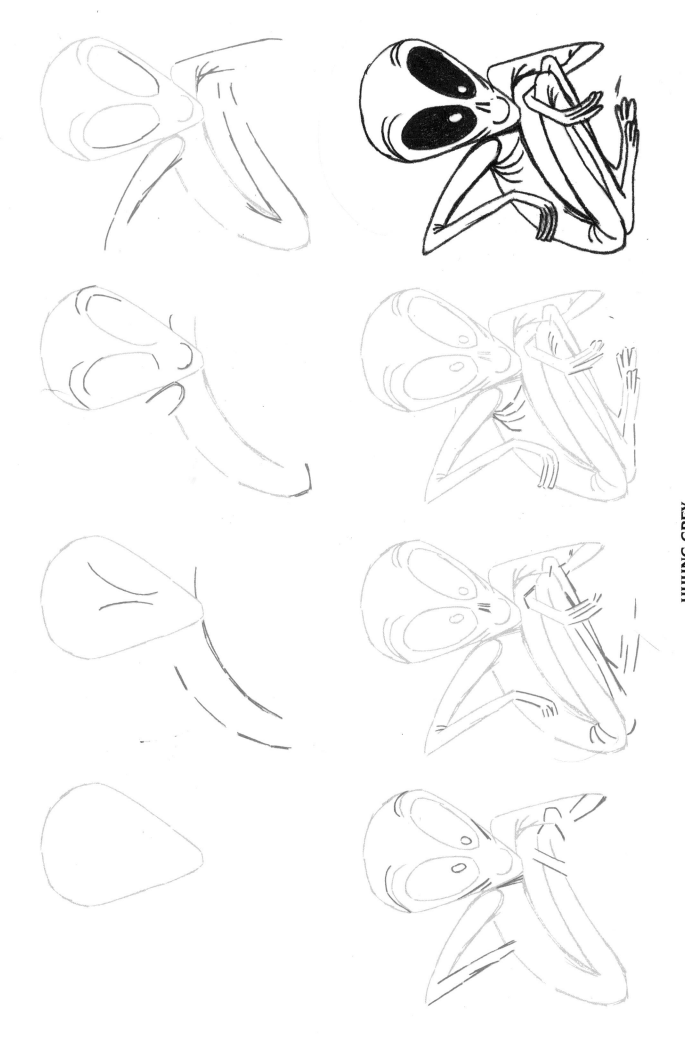

HUHNG GREY
Common gaunt Grey spotted near Route 375 in Arizona. Home unknown.

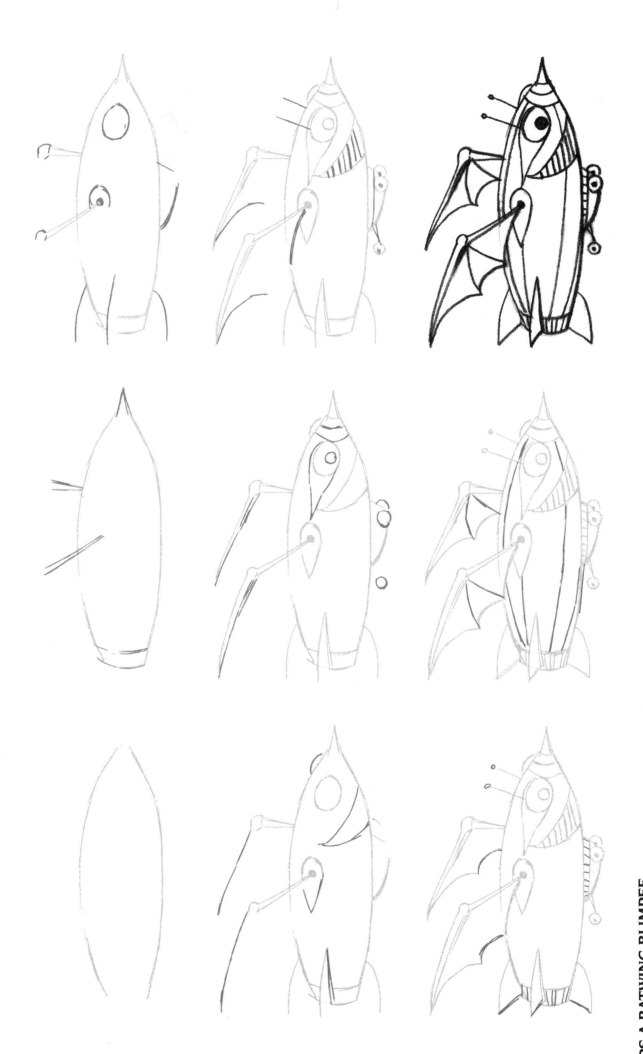

IOT-PS A BATWING BLIMPEE
An Inter-Orbit Ten Passenger Shuttle yet to be discovered.

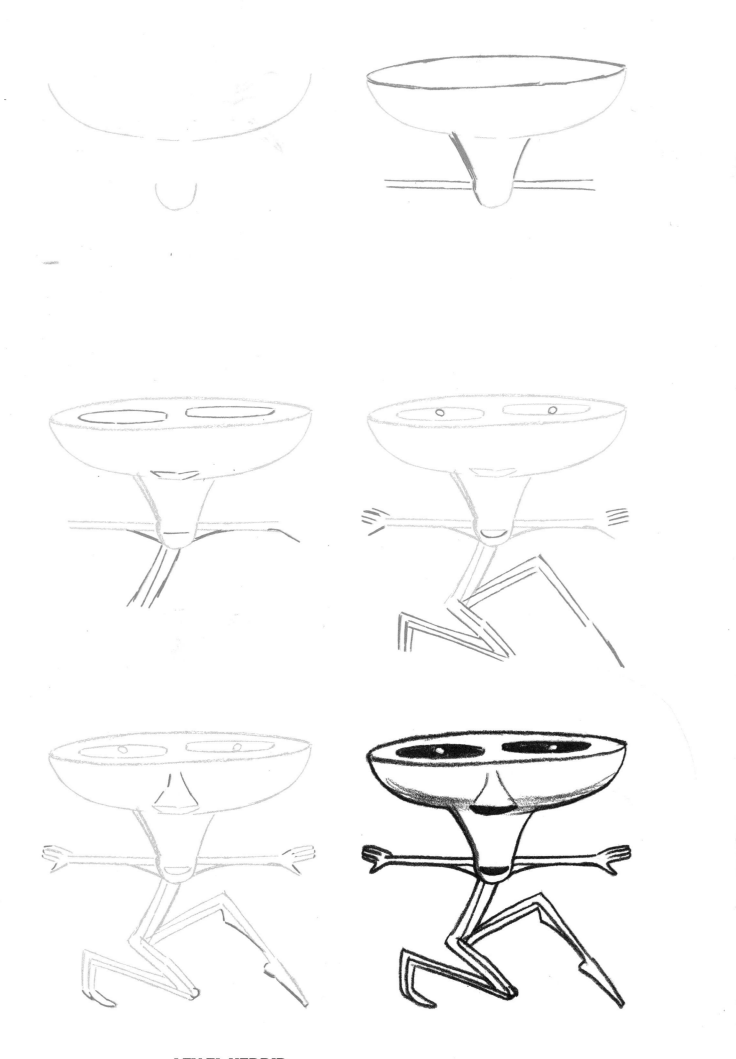

LEV EL HEDDID
Sensible, even-tempered visitor from vicinity of Fum al Samakah.

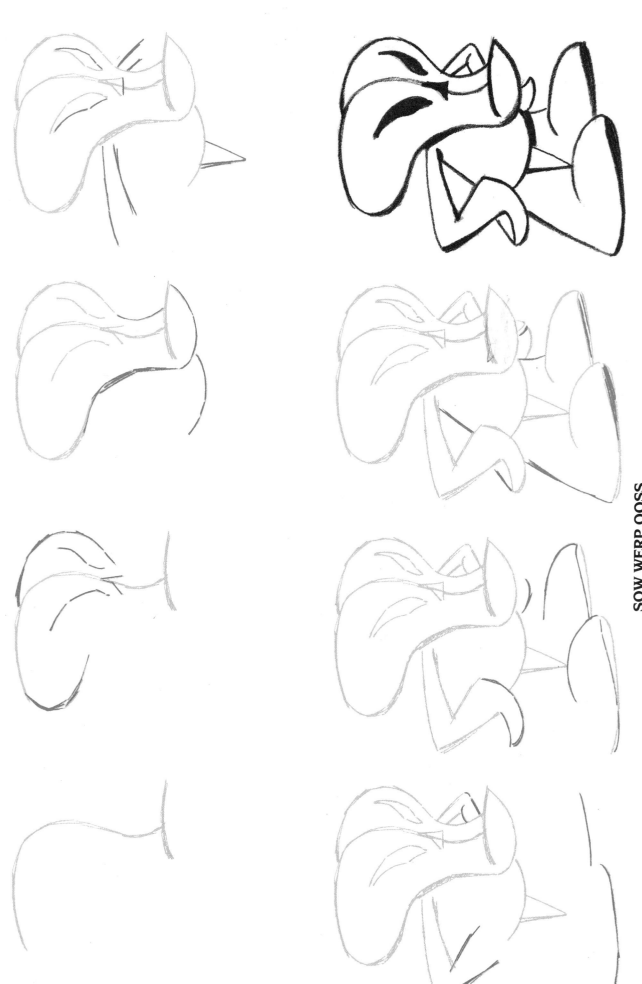

SOW WERP OOSS
Mean-tempered creature reported seen near Groom Lake, Nevada. Home unknown.

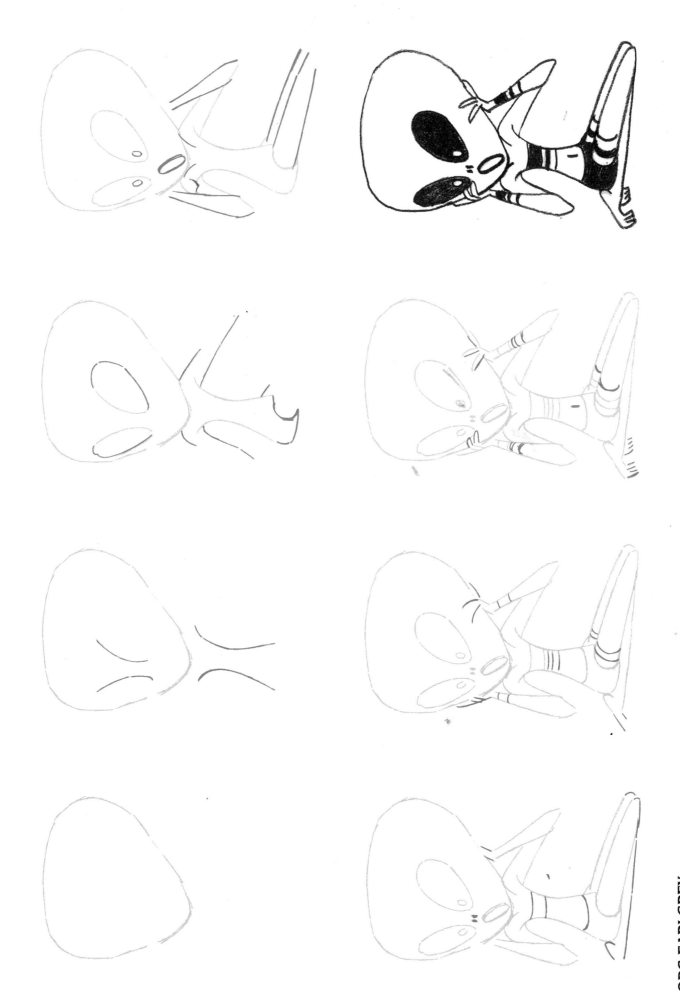

GLAMM OORG EARLGREY
Guest also from Fum al Samakah. Feeds on tea-like nutrient.

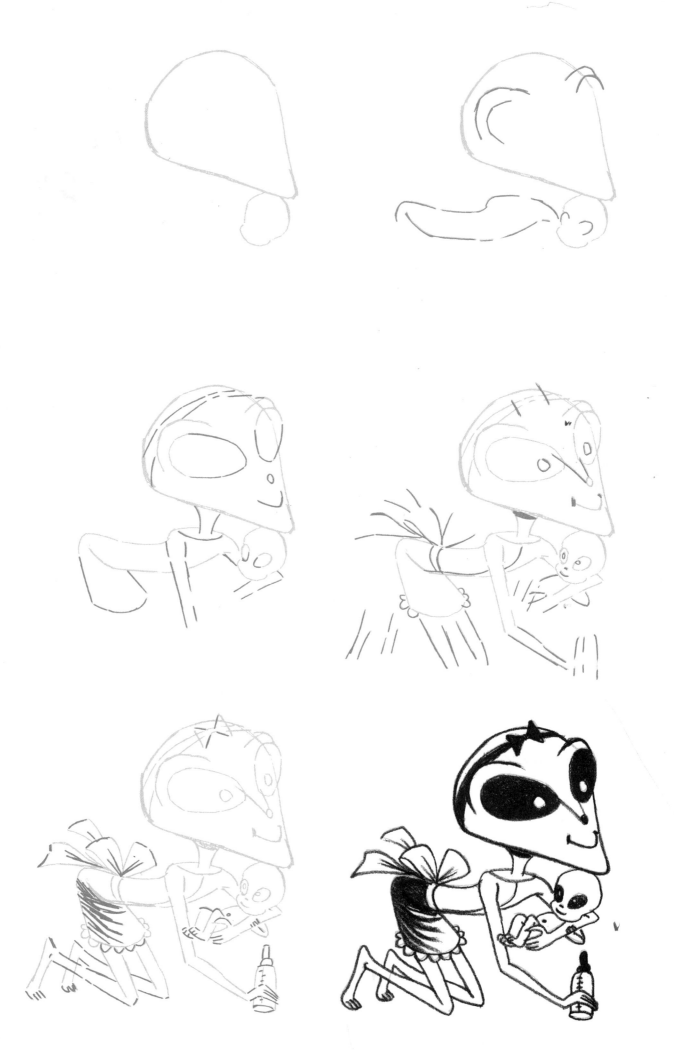

PEARL AND MOTHER OF PEARL
Two Fum al Samakah Pearl Greys.

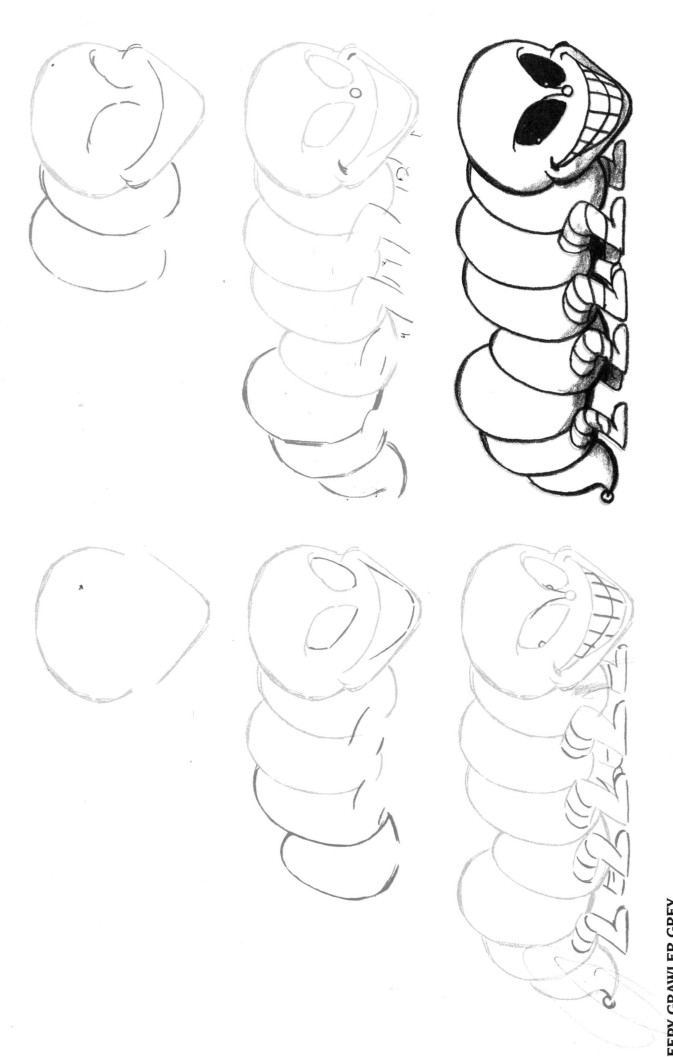

GREEPY GRAWLER GREY
Tiny multiped seen crawling off foot of Sow Werp Ooss.

GALAXY GHOULS

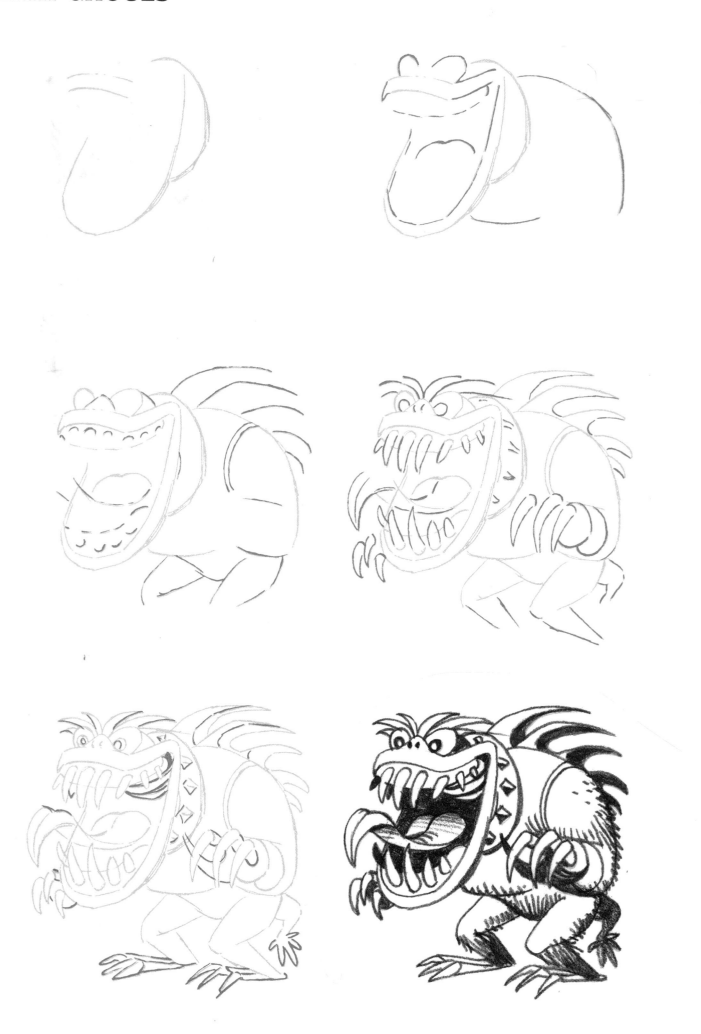

GABBA GHOUL
Ham actor from theater complex in Orion.

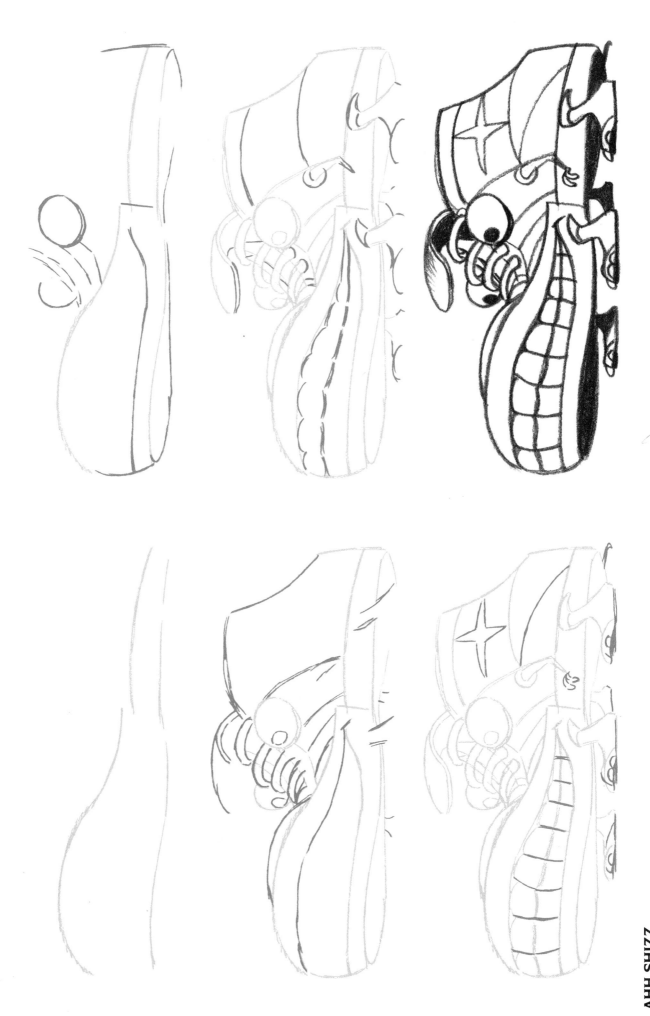

GHOUL AHH SHIZZ
Doomed hiker from unknown frozen region.

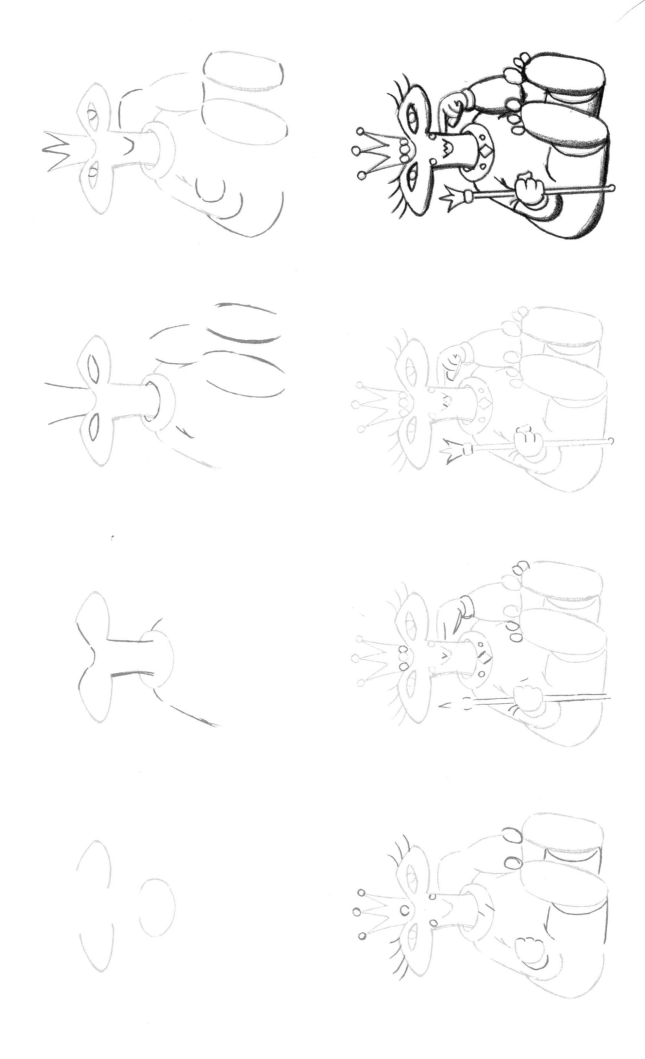

GHOUL DRINKA WATR
Naïve princess of minor Naos planet.

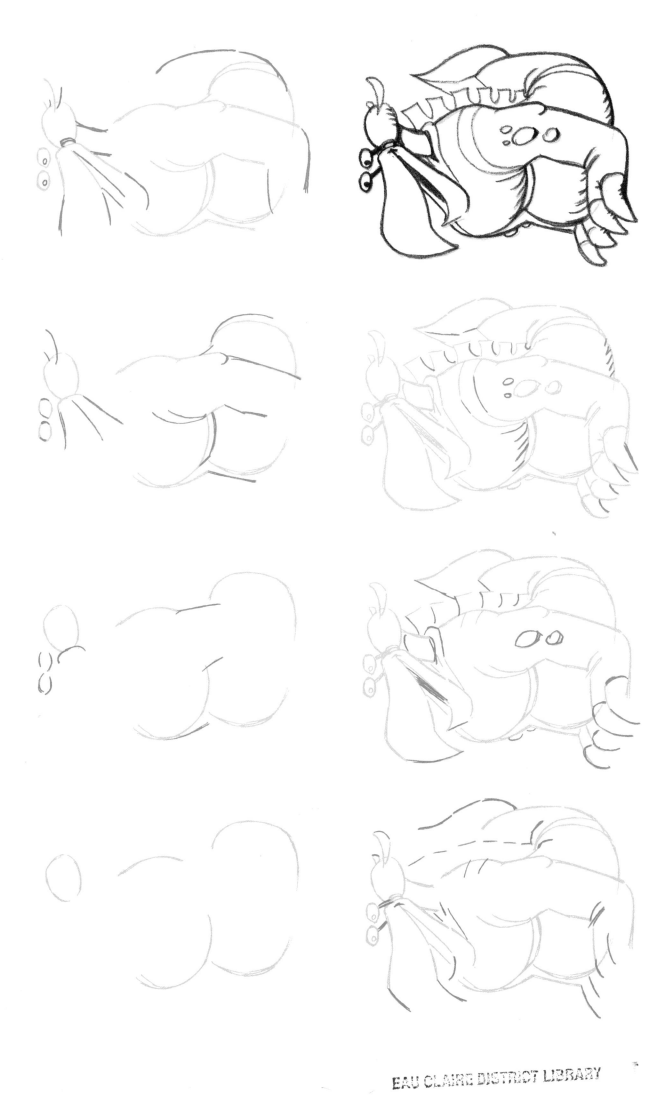

HUHN GHAR YINGHOUL ASH
Peppery tourist from Thuban's fourth planet.

NEBULA NOMADS

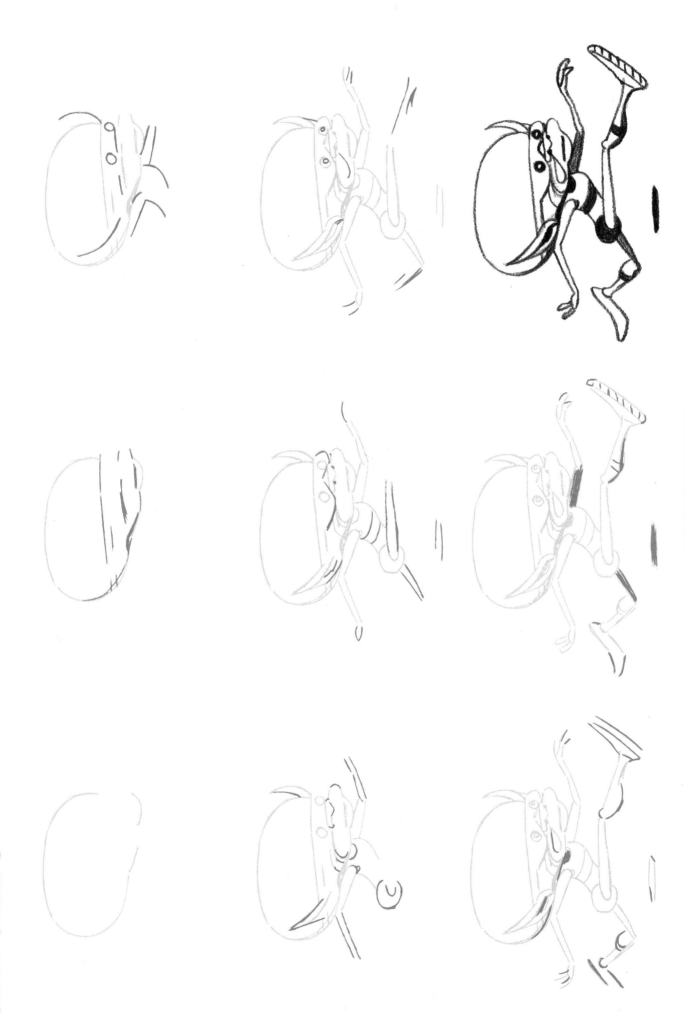

AH YAMMAFAH RUNNER
Champion long-distance runner from neighborhood of Betelgeuse.

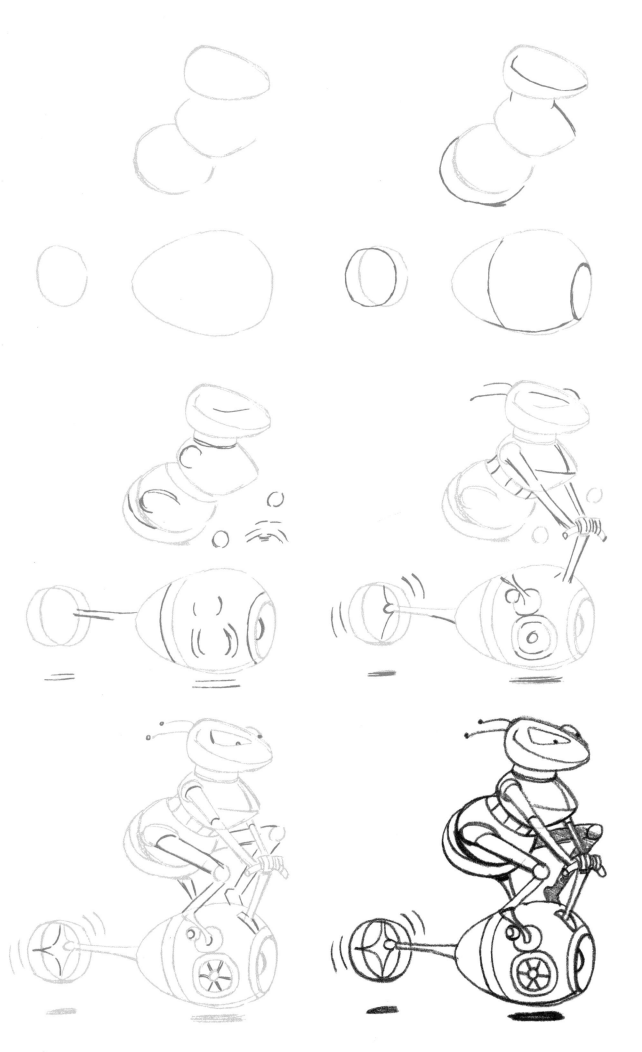

RYE DIMM KA-OOBUOY
Herder of the Porrima star system's food conveyors.

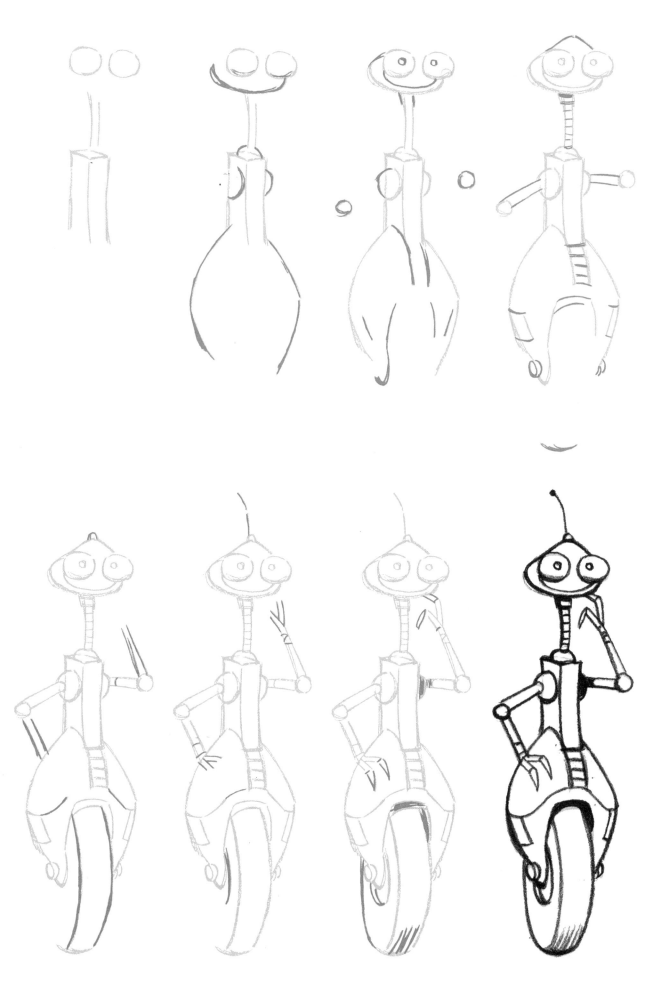

ROHV INGG KA-OOBUOY
Assistant to Rye Dimm Ka-oobuoy.

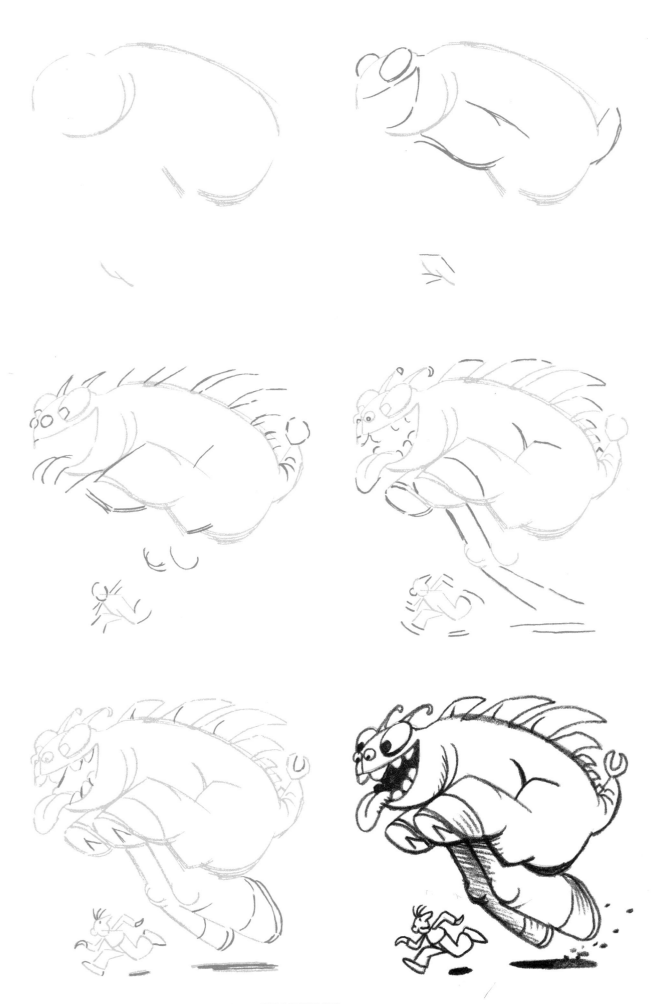

HOPP AHLONG KAZZADEECH
Last friendly nomad from unknown star system observed in the Bronx, New York.

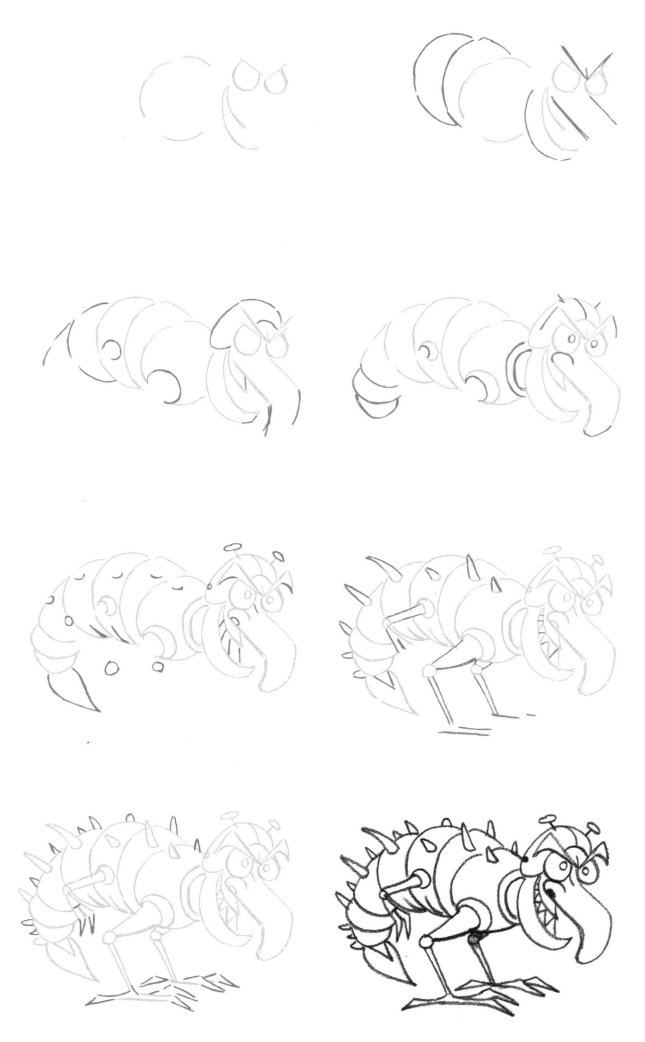

KRIMM INILK ROOK
An escaped, wandering thief from an unknown galaxy penitentiary.

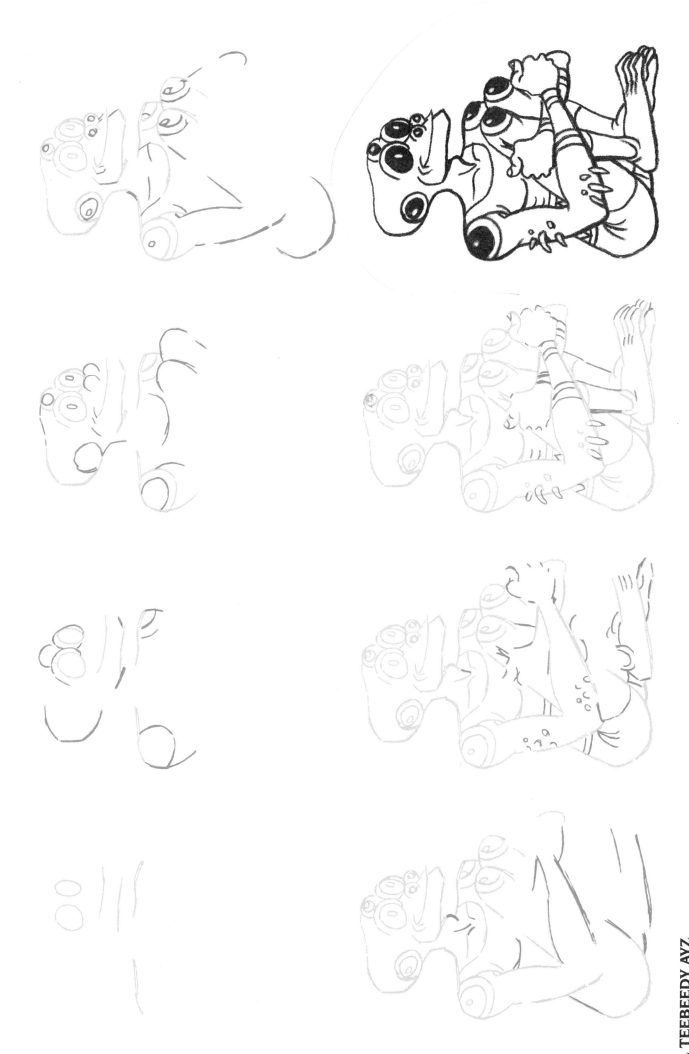

MULL TEEBEEDY AYZ
Interloper from unknown galaxy. All-seeing nomad but dim-witted!

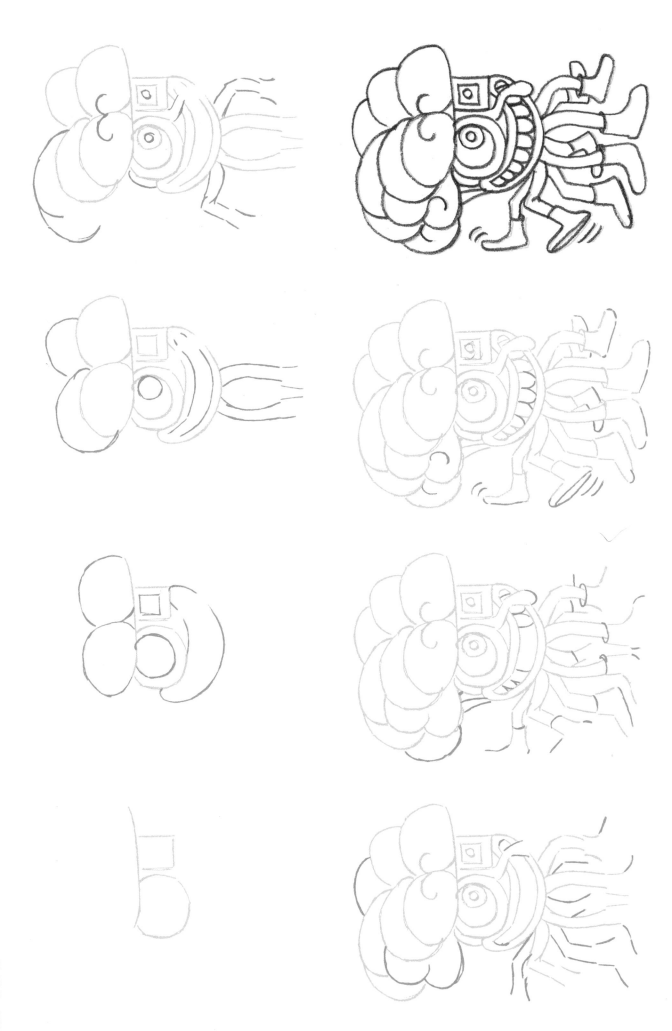

MILKY WAY MARAUDERS

PAH STYOOR AHYZZD
"Purified" native of moon circling third planet of Etamin.

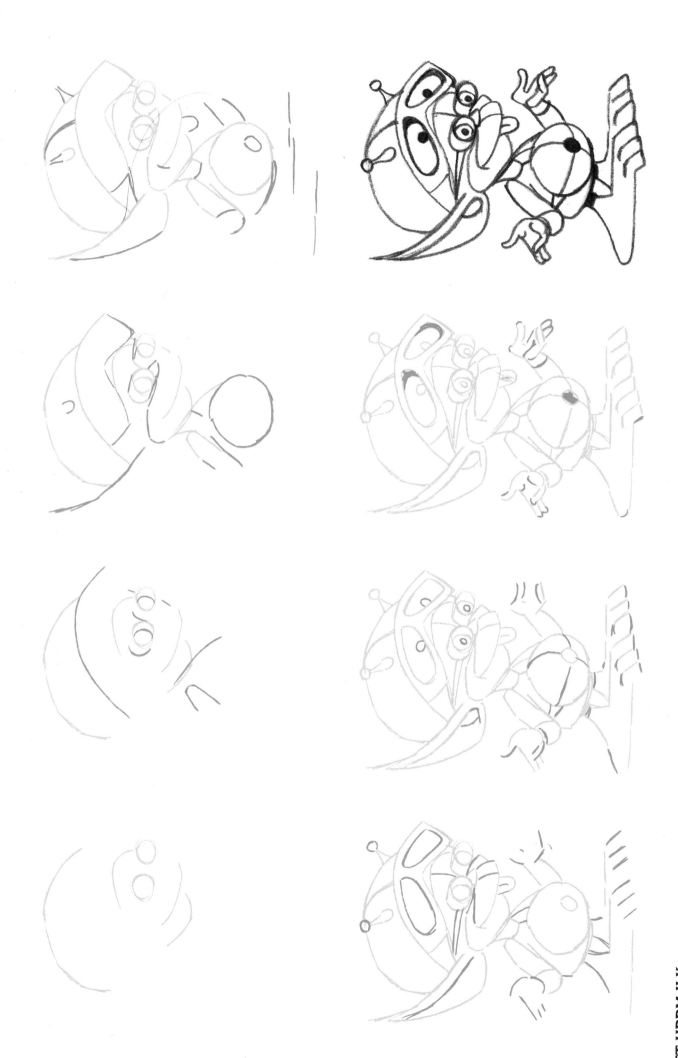

BUHTT URRM ILK
Pale yellow segmented crafty creeper from nebula NGC 2440.

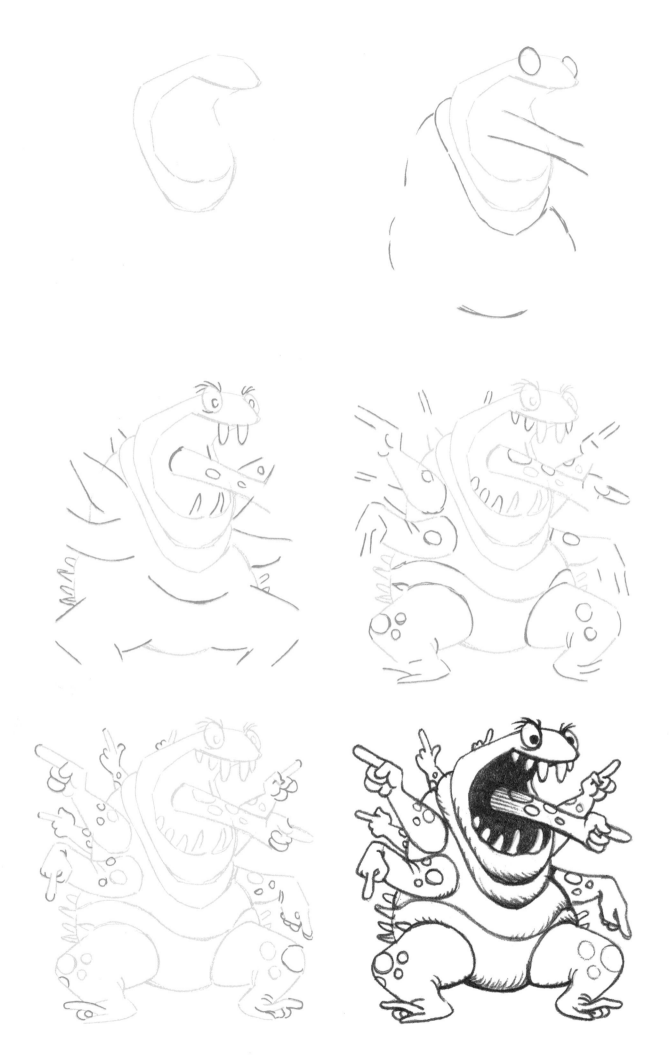

CAM M. BEAR
Foul-smelling tongue pointer from the Little Dumbbell nebula.

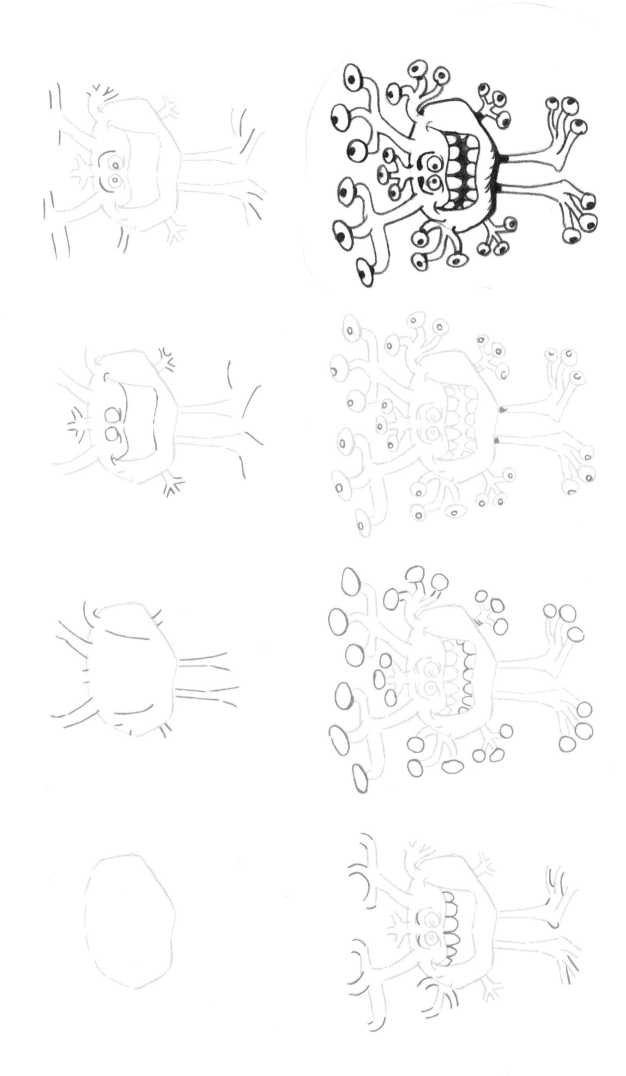

MUTTZARR ELLAH
Stringy parolee from a Tania Borealis reformatory.

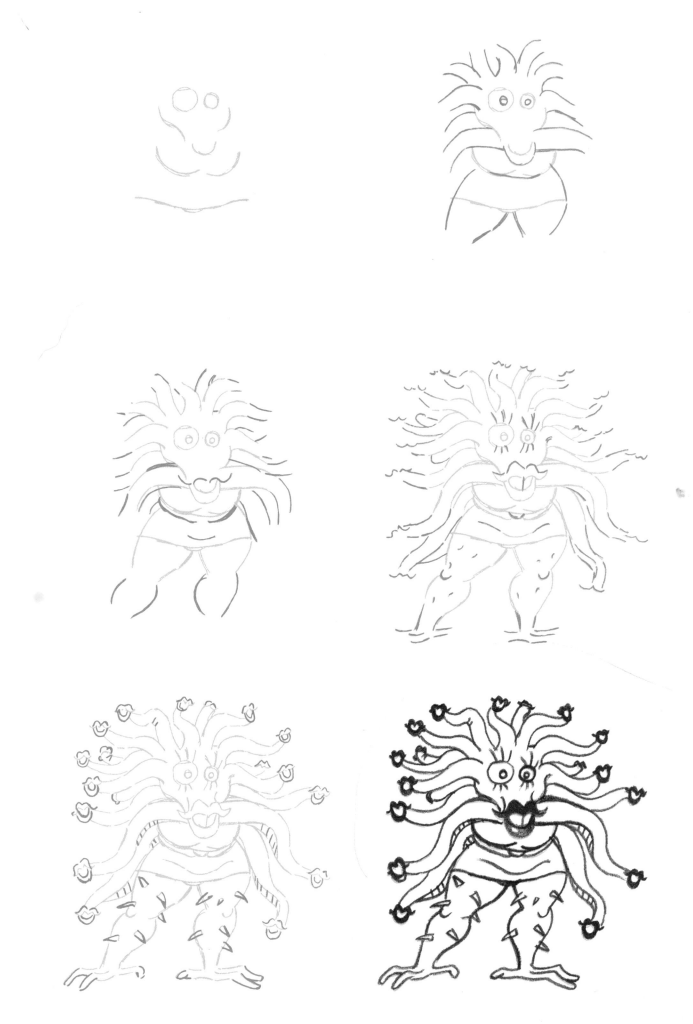

PAR MIZH AHN
A relative of Muttzarr Ellah.

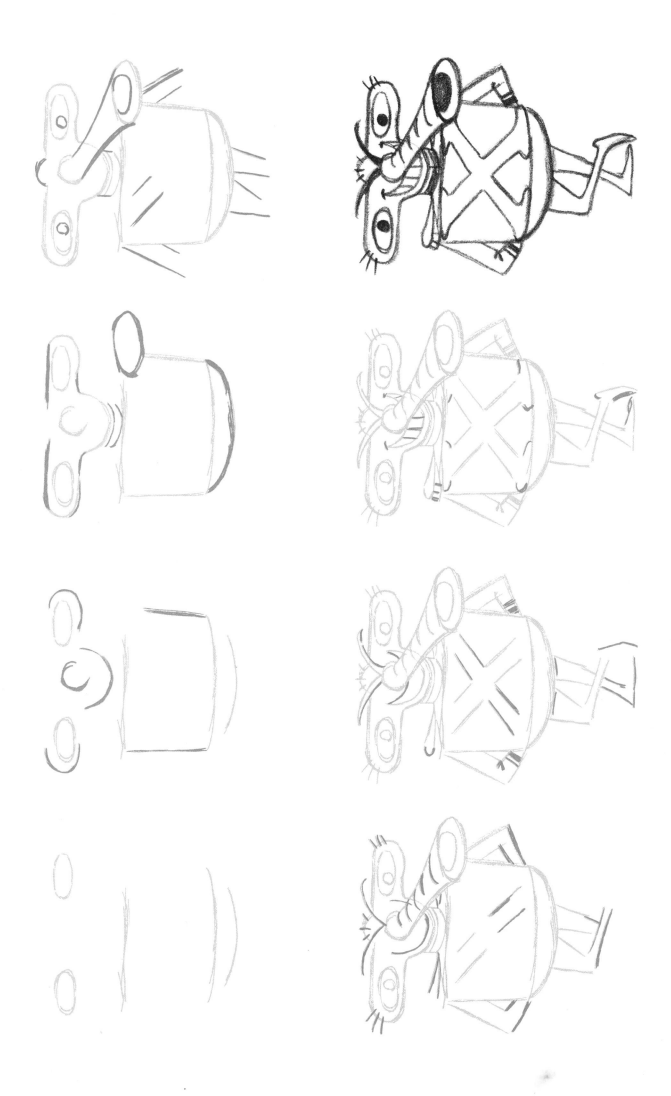

FEYT AHCH EEZ
An "old salt" from the El Nath star system.

P. CHIZZANK REEM
Very pleasant organism with a sweet smile found in our galaxy.

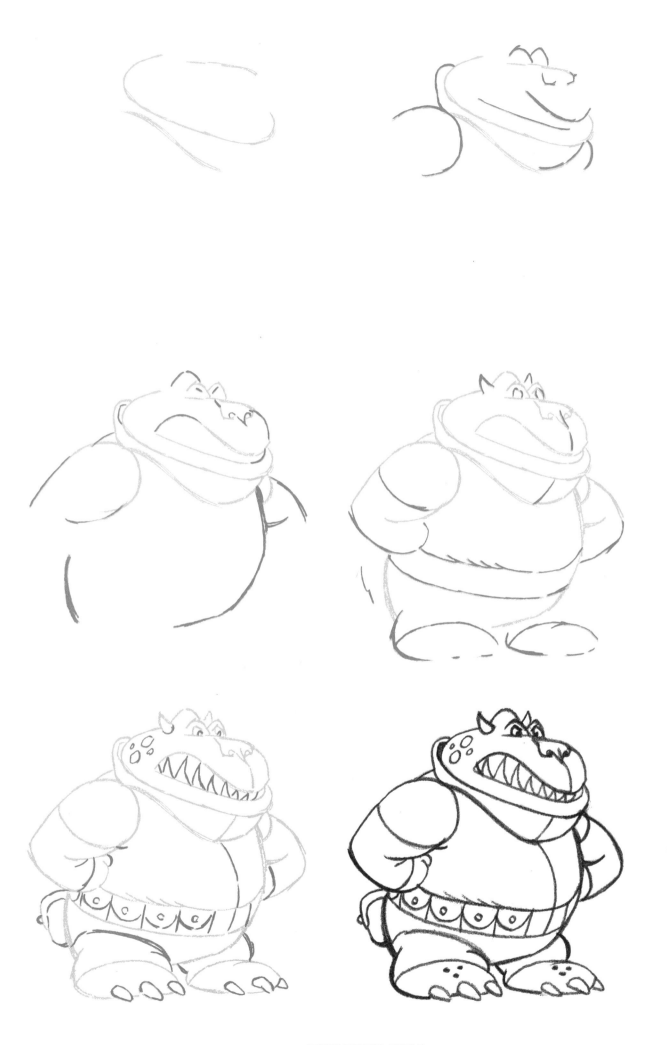

BUH TURB AWLL
Noisy, fatty visitor from one of Antares' planets.

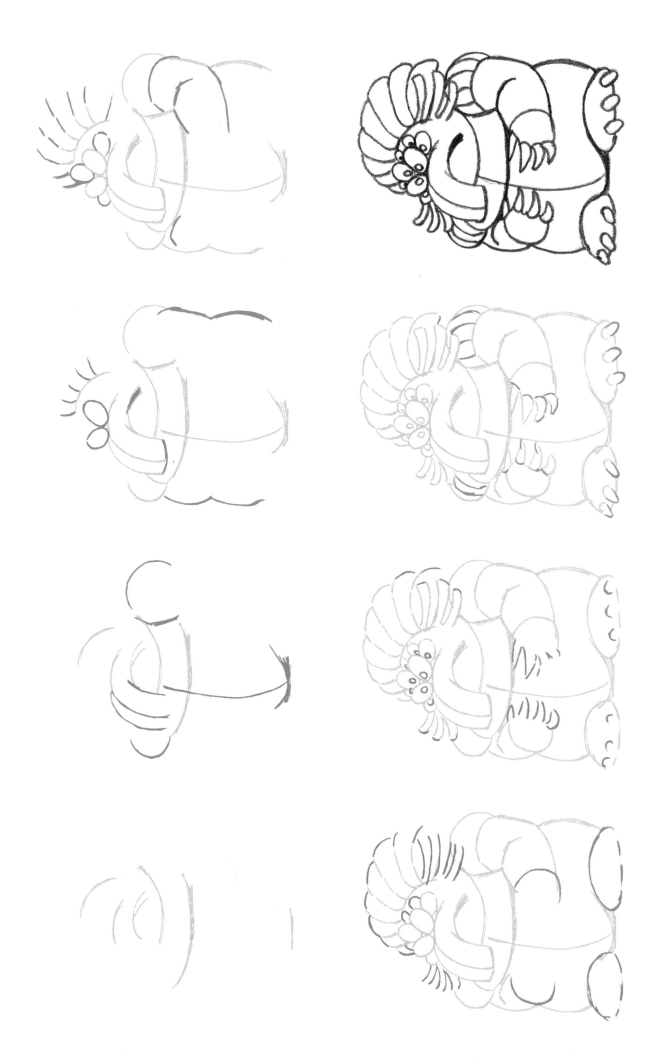

GORGHONN ZOLA
Smelly, savory, spaced-out nanny.

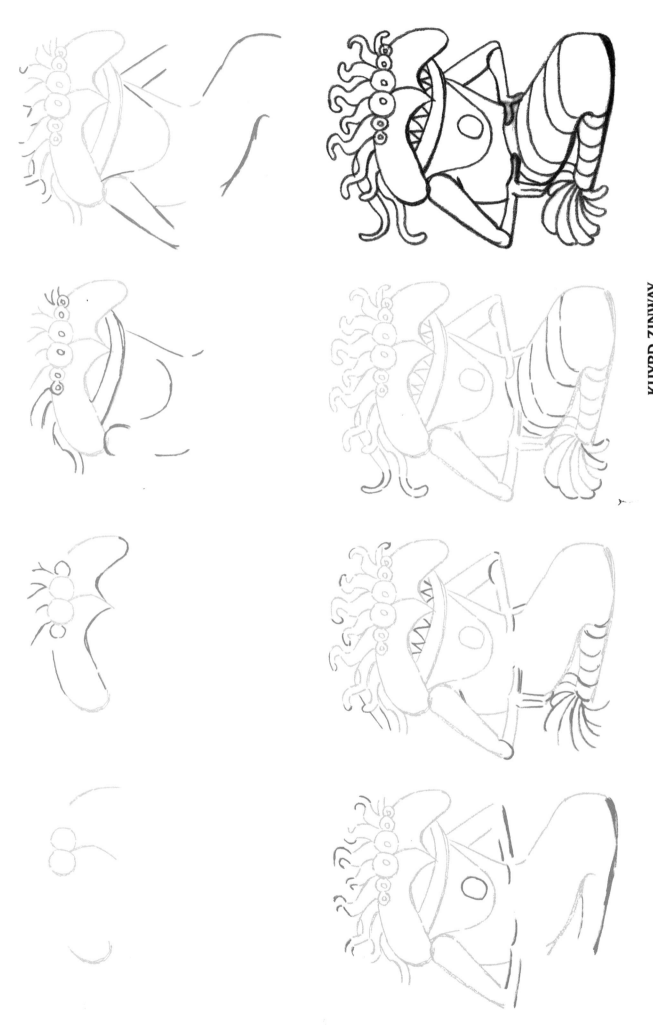

KUYRD ZINWAY
Split personality from planet orbiting Angetenar.

KAHFI YISE KREEM
A luscious, keyed-up guest from the vicinity of the star Vega.

COSMIC MARAUDERS

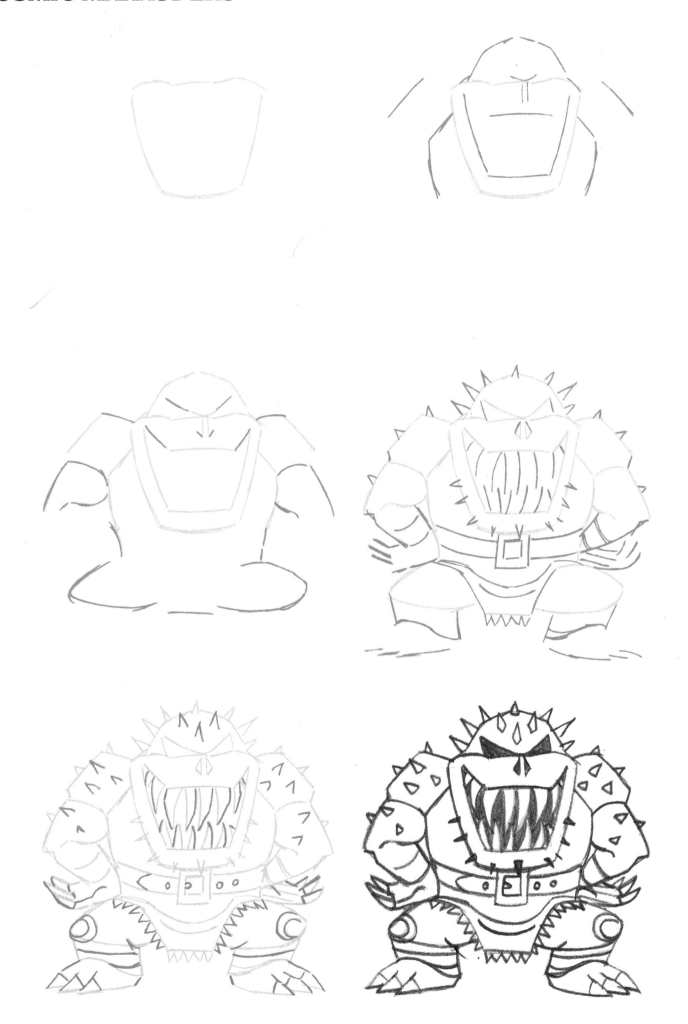

DEE PROOOTCANN AL
The terrible, toothy tickler from an unknown planet in the Eskimo nebula.

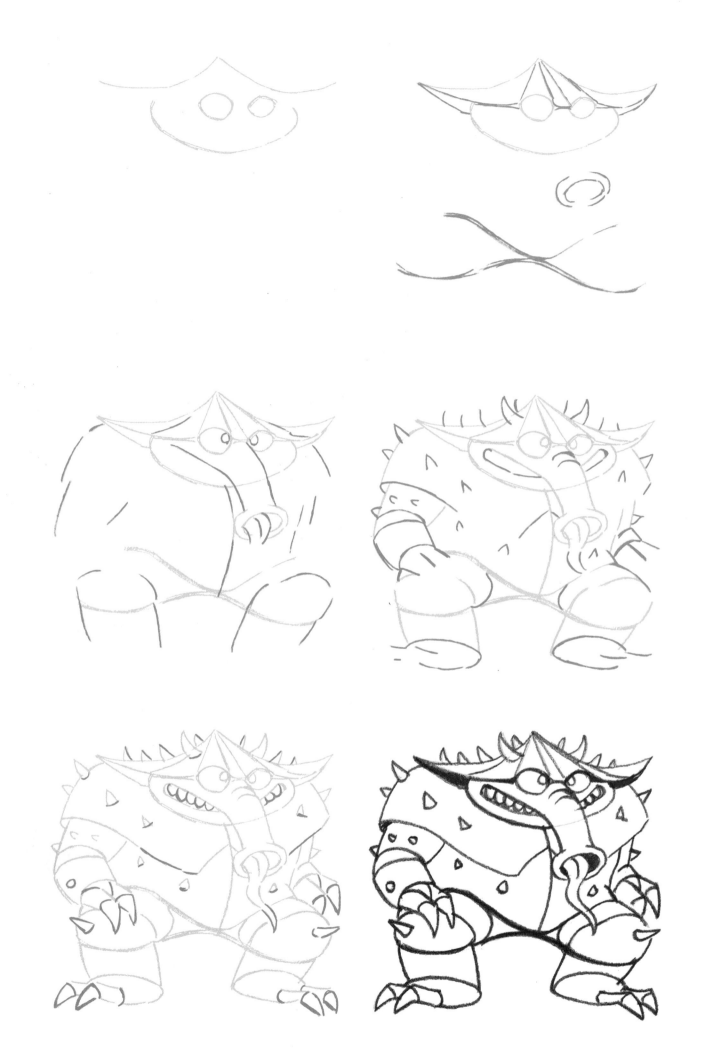

NAYZZEL LIKKINHULK
A savage from the environment of the Oort cloud.

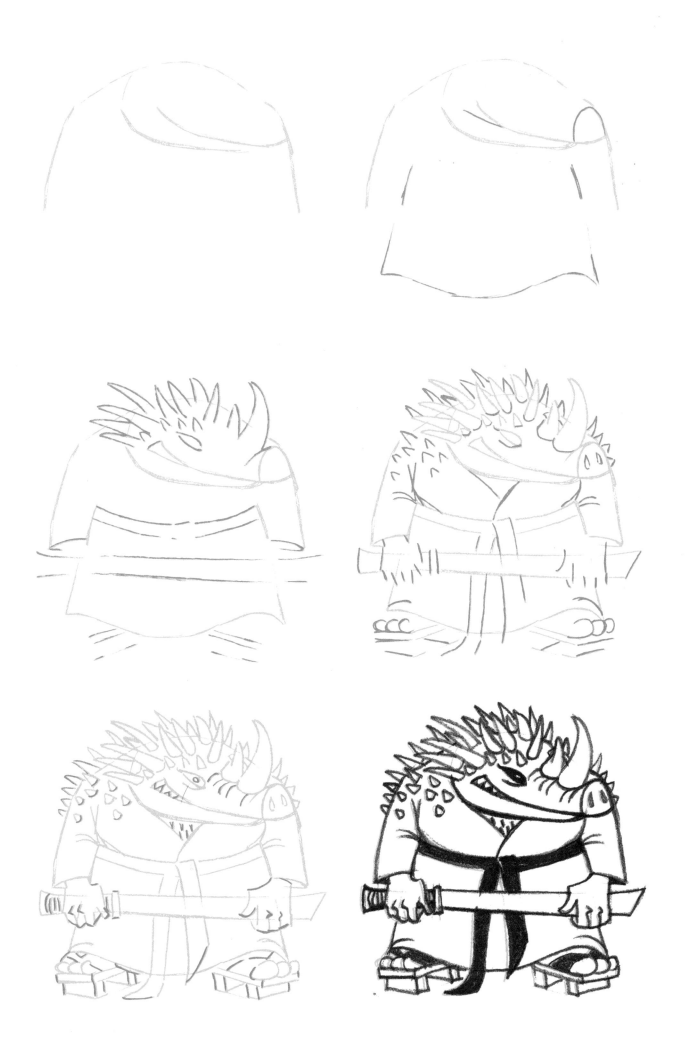

HAKK IMUPPIN WEEBITZ
The horrible hacker from the Horsehead galaxy.

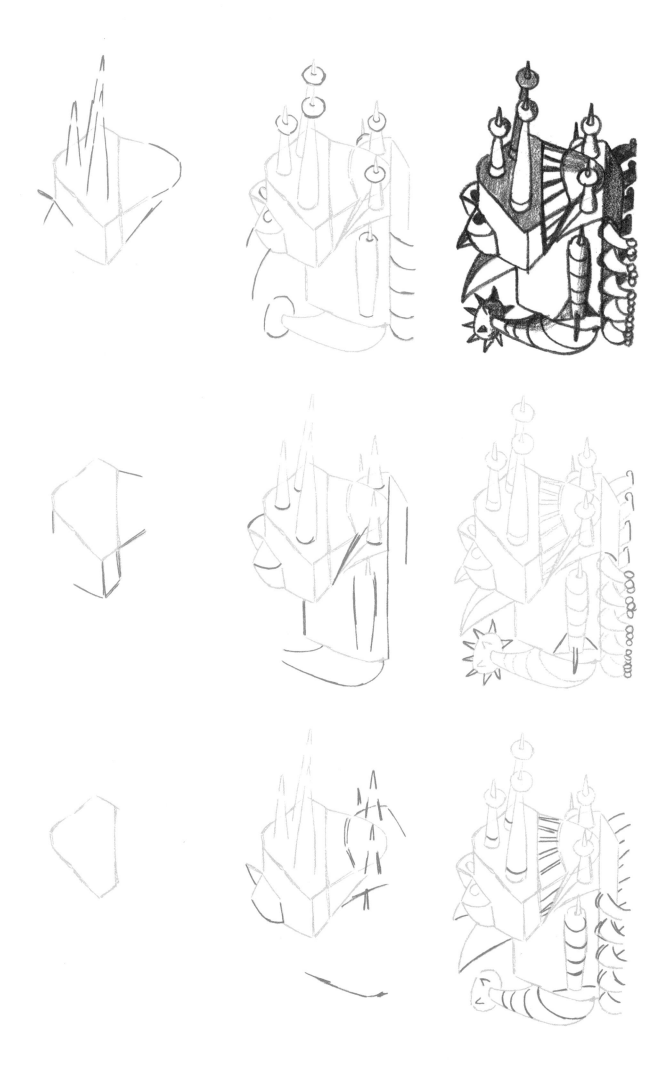

GUNGALORE SENTIPEEDUS
A "hired gun" from the constellation Cassiopeia.

ETCs (EXTRATERRESTRIAL CURIOSITIES)

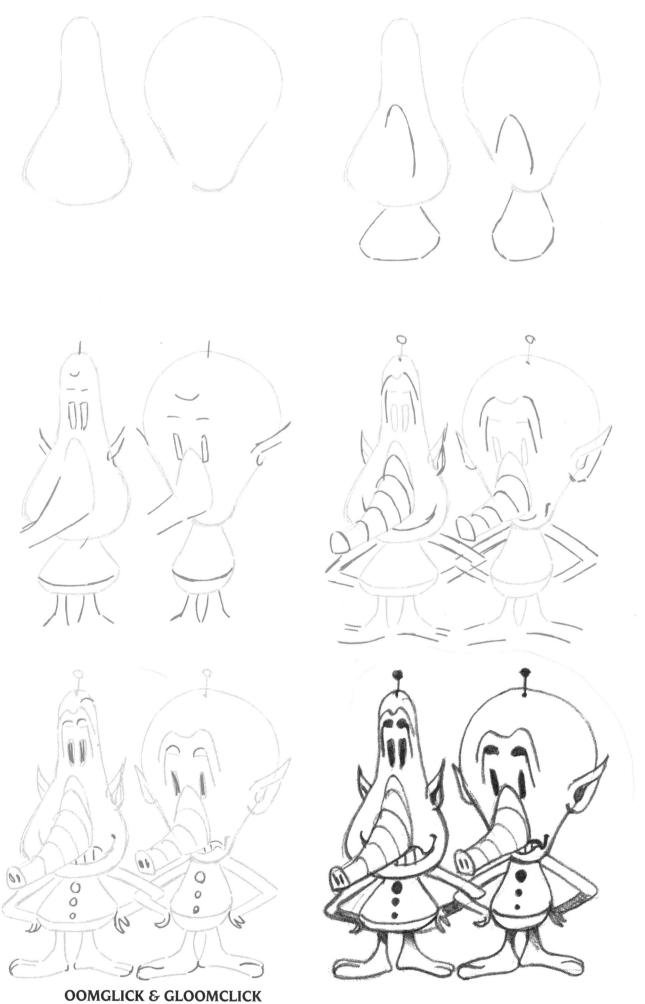

OOMGLICK & GLOOMCLICK
Orphans, fraternal, trunk-nosed twins, from locality of an unknown dwarf star.

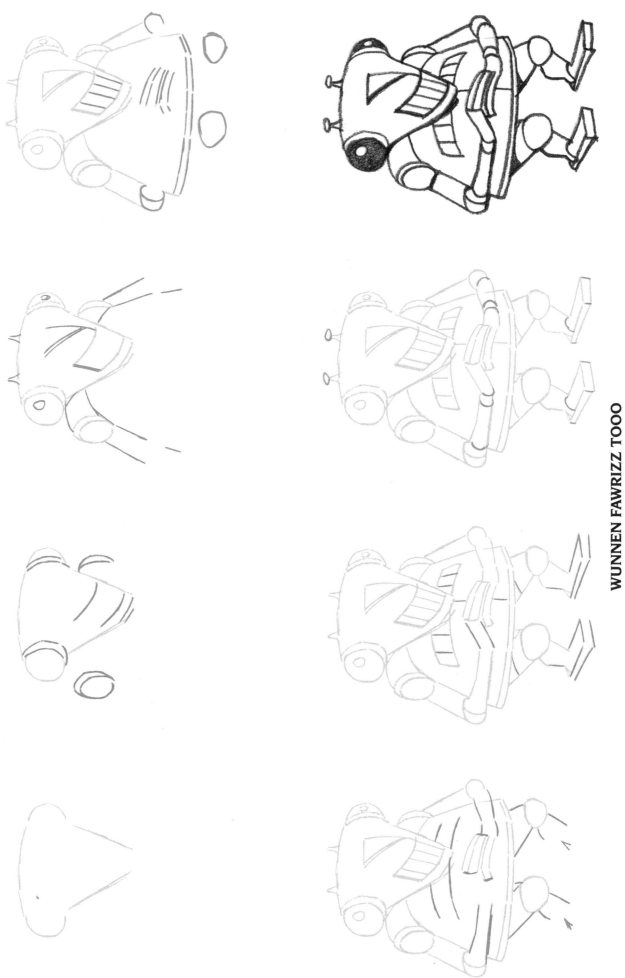

WUNNEN FAWRIZZ TOOO
Wunnens are notoriously poor in arithmetic. They are found on the planet of Zosma.

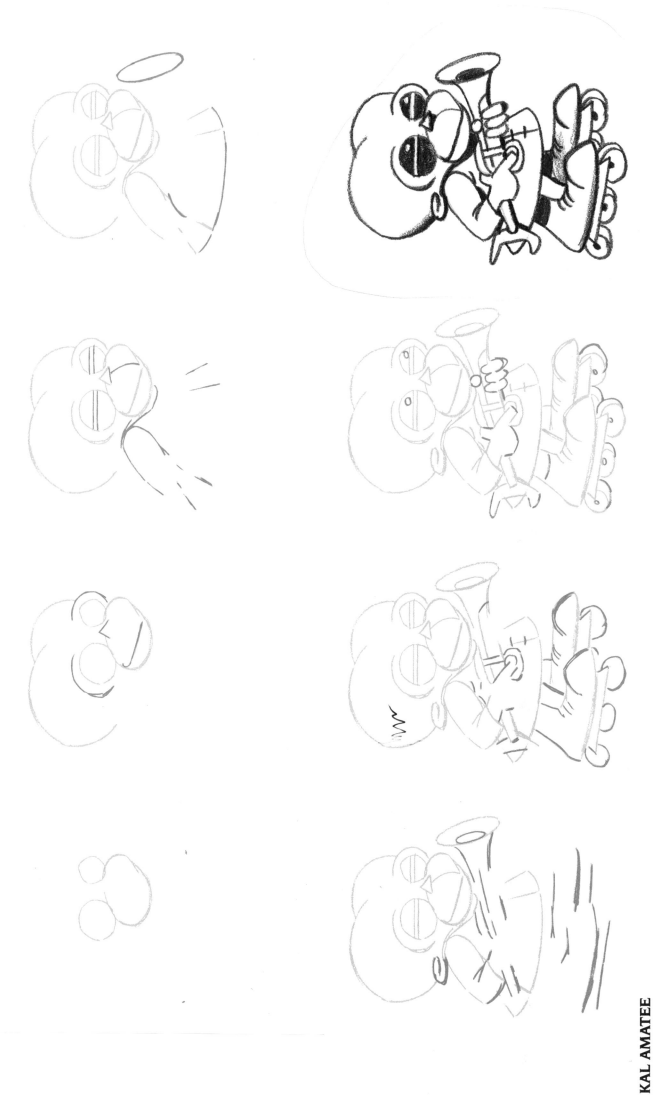

KAL AMATEE
Pear-headed tramp with blunderbuss-like weapon. Native of planet circling Nodus Secundus.

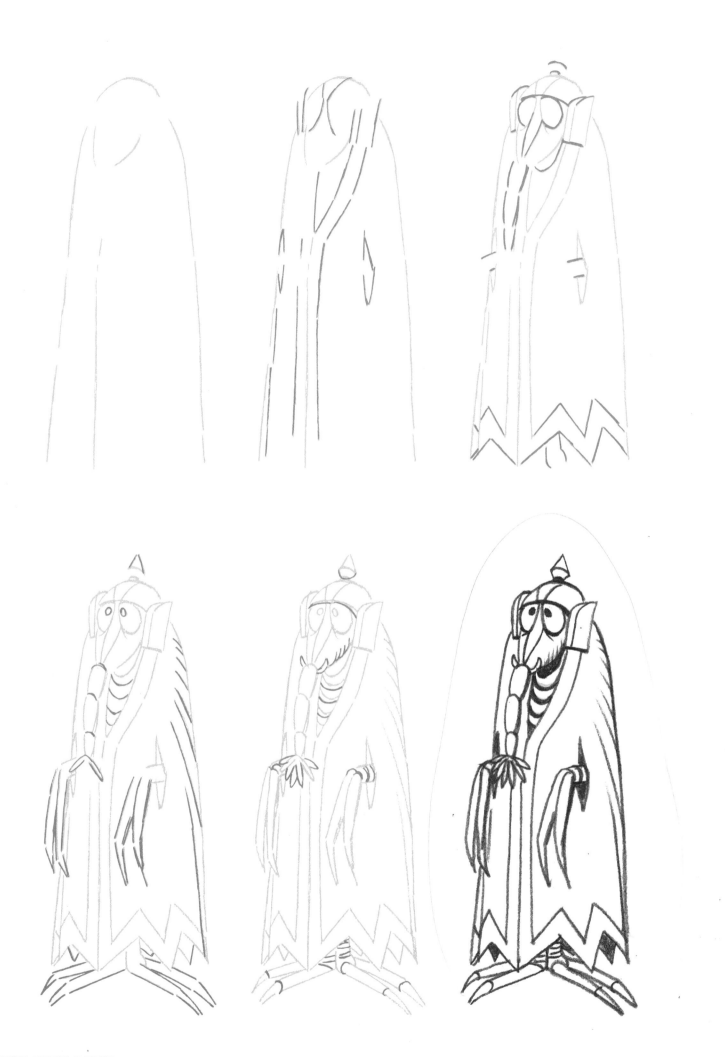

MAJOR DIZZ ASTIR
Woeful spike-headed wimp from Tania Australis.

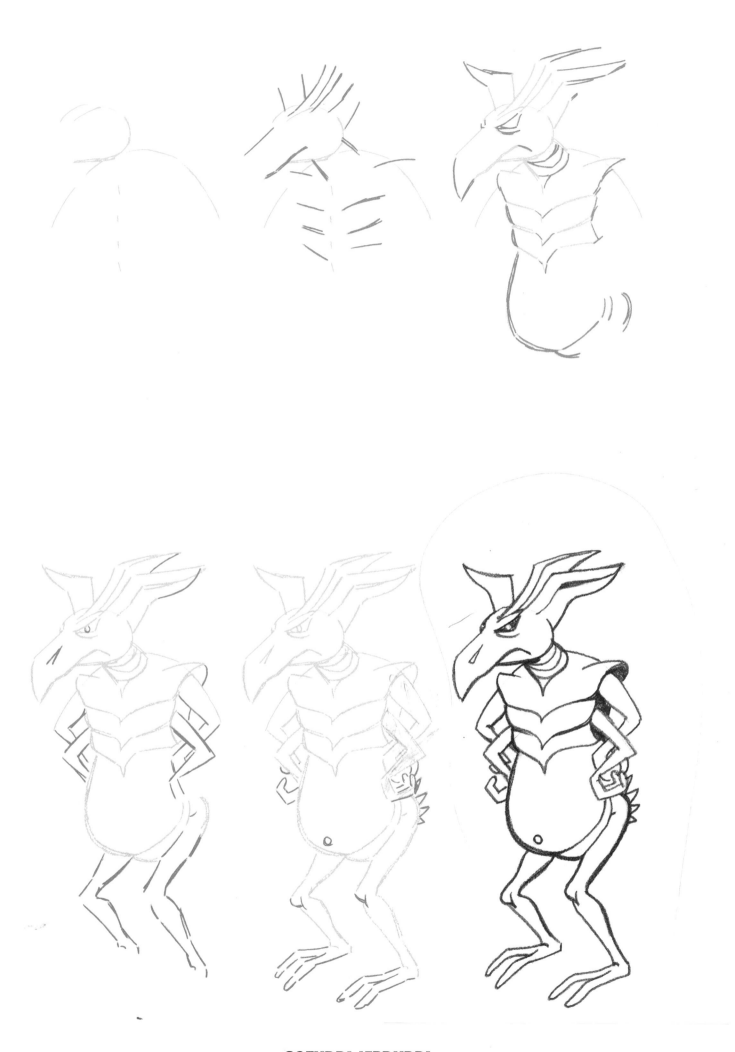

GOFUDDL YIRDUDDL
Common insulting driggo out of the Tejat Posterior.

AITCH EYE JAYKAYE
A domesticated Jaykaye; common pet found in the Little Dumbbell nebula.

LAKOO KAROTSHA
Tiny vermin pest unearthed on remote planet in the Crab nebula.

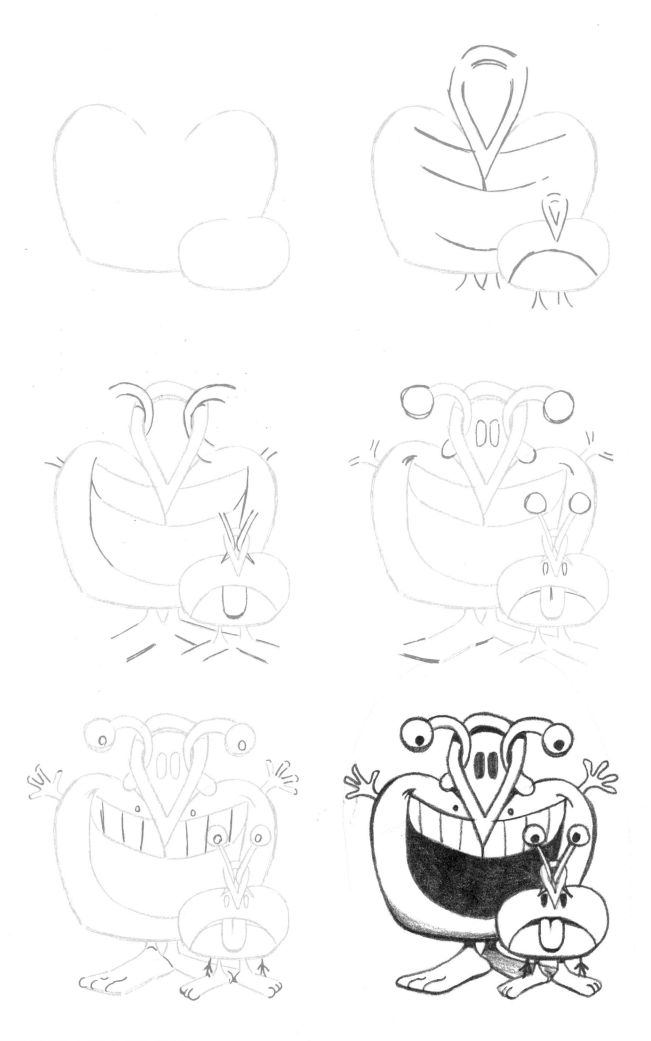

GOGGLE GLEE & GOGGLE GLUM
Green gobloons from Grus.

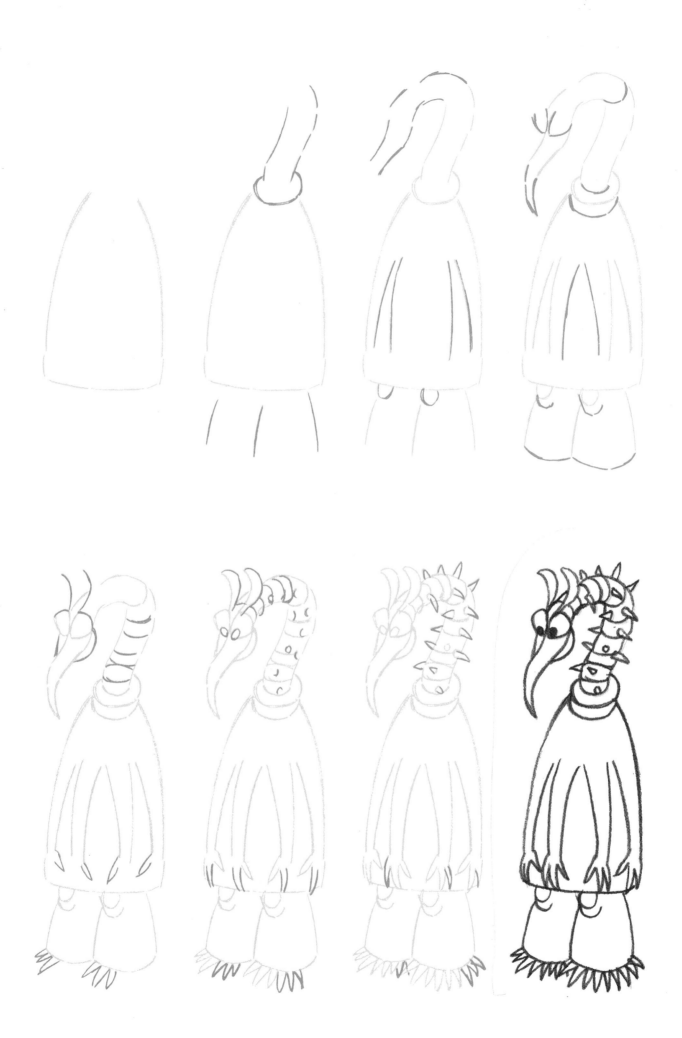

STUMM EHKAKE
A spike-necked gork from the constellation Aquarius.

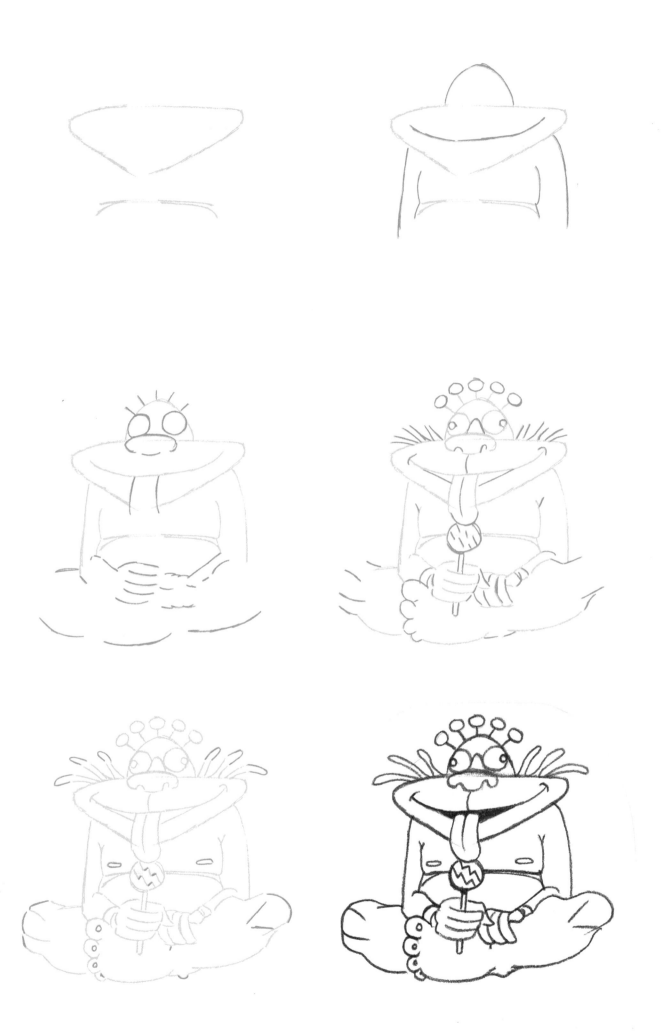

ELL LEMON OHPEE
Far-out comedian performing in amusement park near Yed Prior.

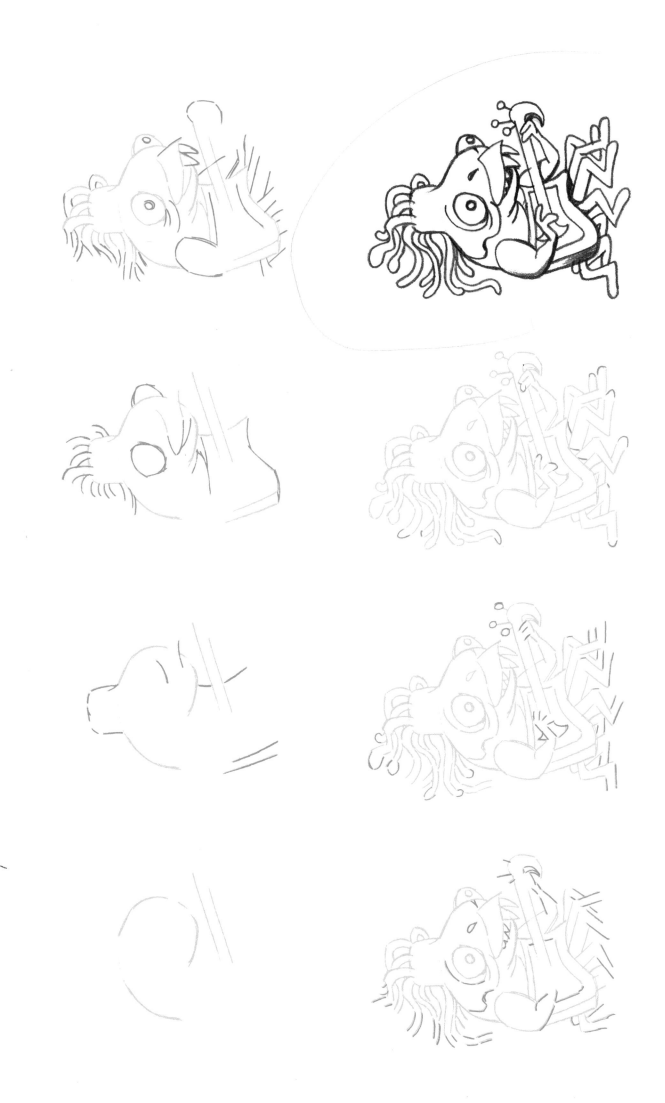

ZKIPP TOOM ALLOO
Homeless troubador from nebula in Orion.

SHMOOTZIK
Unsanitary denizen of moon of third planet of Grumium.

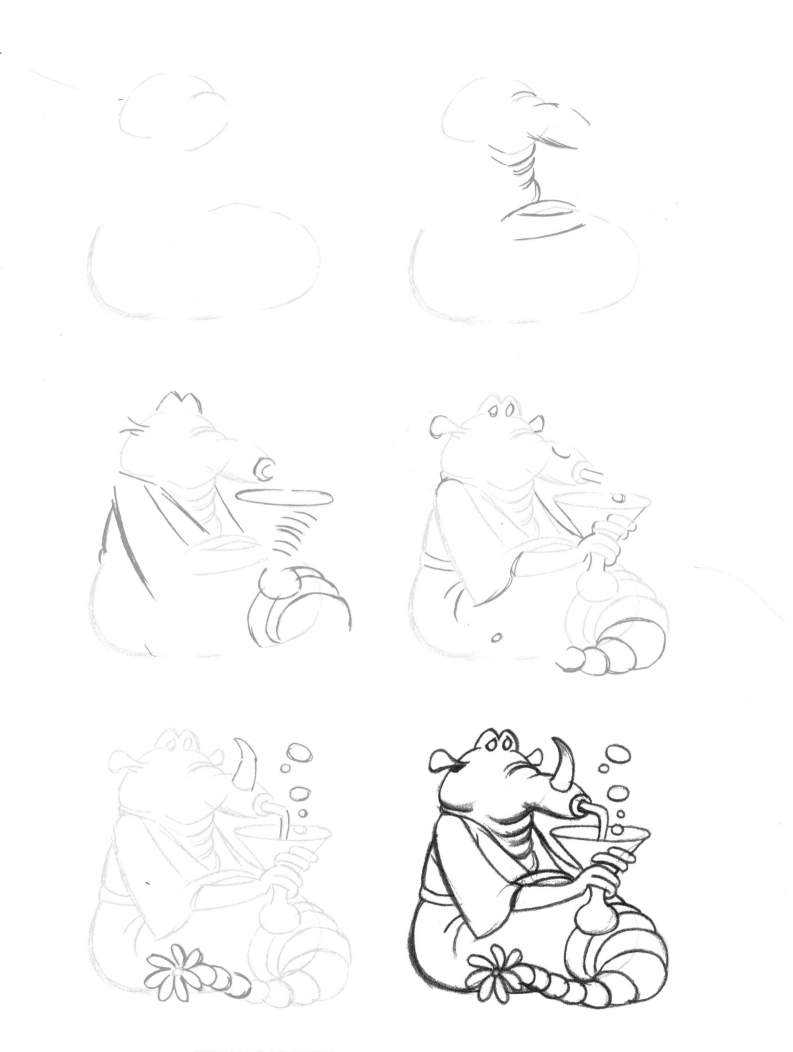

STUMBLE RILTZKIN
Seltzer sucker from carbonated water planet in Gacrux star system.

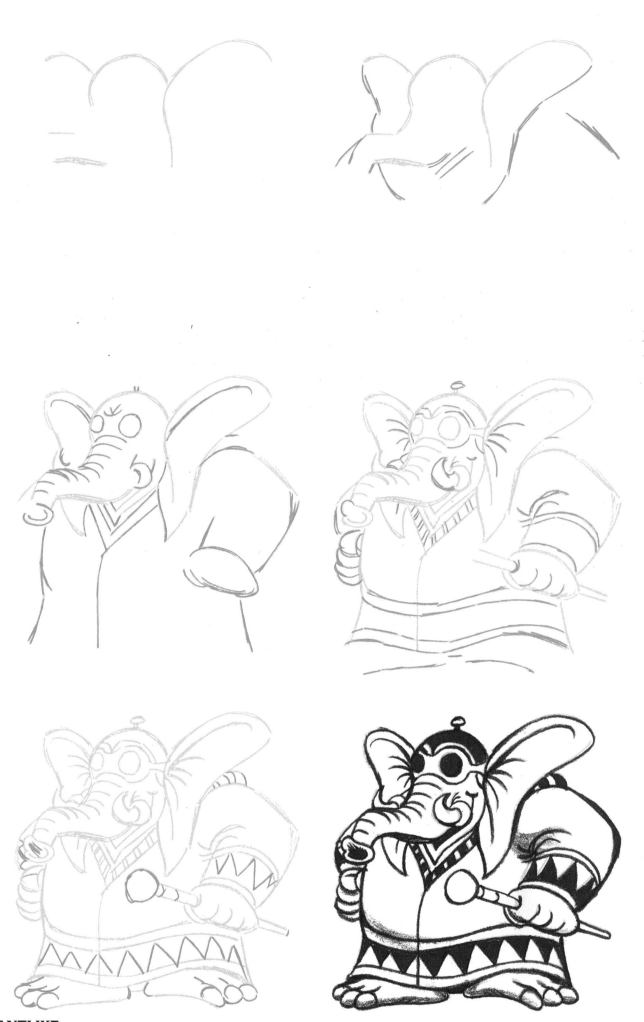

ELL F ANTLIKE

Resembles our African pachyderm but is very, very tiny. Blows poison fumes from its wee trunk. Native of a Tyl planet.

Using Lee J. Ames's proven, step-by-step method of drawing instruction you can easily learn to draw animals, monsters, airplanes, cars, sharks, buildings, dinosaurs, famous cartoons, and so much more! Millions of people have learned to draw by using the award-winning "Draw 50" technique. Now you can too!

COLLECT THE ENTIRE DRAW 50 SERIES!

The Draw 50 Series books are available from your local bookstore.
You may also order direct (make a copy of this form to order).
Titles are paperback, unless otherwise indicated.

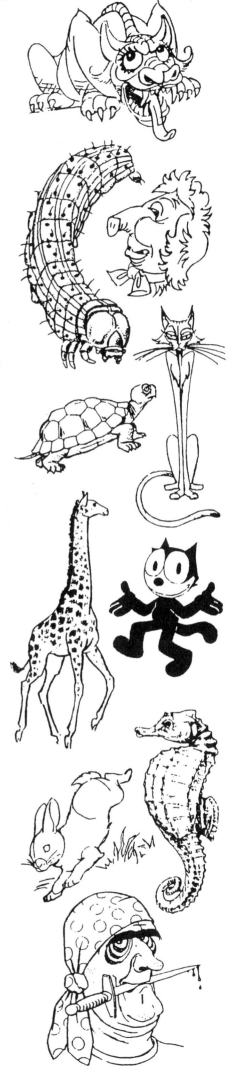

ISBN	TITLE	PRICE	QTY	TOTAL
23629-8	Airplanes, Aircraft, and Spacecraft	$8.95/$11.95 Can	× _____	= _____
49145-X	Aliens	$8.95/$11.95 Can	× _____	= _____
19519-2	Animals	$8.95/$11.95 Can	× _____	= _____
24638-2	Athletes	$8.95/$11.95 Can	× _____	= _____
26767-3	Beasties and Yugglies and Turnover Uglies and Things That Go Bump in the Night	$8.95/$11.95 Can	× _____	= _____
47163-7	Birds	$8.95/$11.95 Can	× _____	= _____
47006-1	Birds (hardcover)	$13.95/$18.95 Can	× _____	= _____
23630-1	Boats, Ships, Trucks and Trains	$8.95/$11.95 Can	× _____	= _____
41777-2	Buildings and Other Structures	$8.95/$11.95 Can	× _____	= _____
24639-0	Cars, Trucks, and Motorcycles	$8.95/$11.95 Can	× _____	= _____
24640-4	Cats	$8.95/$11.95 Can	× _____	= _____
42449-3	Creepy Crawlies	$8.95/$11.95 Can	× _____	= _____
19520-6	Dinosaurs and Other Prehistoric Animals	$8.95/$11.95 Can	× _____	= _____
23431-7	Dogs	$8.95/$11.95 Can	× _____	= _____
46985-3	Endangered Animals	$8.95/$11.95 Can	× _____	= _____
19521-4	Famous Cartoons	$8.95/$11.95 Can	× _____	= _____
23432-5	Famous Faces	$8.95/$11.95 Can	× _____	= _____
47150-5	Flowers, Trees, and Other Plants	$8.95/$11.95 Can	× _____	= _____
26770-3	Holiday Decorations	$8.95/$11.95 Can	× _____	= _____
17642-2	Horses	$8.95/$11.95 Can	× _____	= _____
17639-2	Monsters	$8.95/$11.95 Can	× _____	= _____
41194-4	People	$8.95/$11.95 Can	× _____	= _____
47162-9	People of the Bible	$8.95/$11.95 Can	× _____	= _____
47005-3	People of the Bible (hardcover)	$13.95/$19.95 Can	× _____	= _____
26768-1	Sharks, Whales, and Other Sea Creatures	$8.95/$11.95 Can	× _____	= _____
14154-8	Vehicles	$8.95/$11.95 Can	× _____	= _____
	Shipping and handling	**(add $2.50 per order)**	× _____	= _____
		TOTAL		_____

Please send me the title(s) I have indicated above. I am enclosing $_____.
Send check or money order in U.S. funds only (no C.O.D.s or cash, please.) Make check payable to Bantam Doubleday Dell. Allow 4–6 weeks for delivery.
Prices and availability subject to change without notice.

Name: _____

Address: _____ Apt. #_____

City: _____ State: _____ Zip: _____

Send completed coupon and payment to:
Bantam Doubleday Dell
ATTN: Distribution Services